THE BONES OF JOSEPH

Gareth Lloyd Jones

The Bones of Joseph

From the Ancient Texts
to the Modern Church

Studies in the Scriptures

WILLIAM B. EERDMANS PUBLISHING COMPANY
GRAND RAPIDS, MICHIGAN / CAMBRIDGE, U.K.

8/0-

© 1997 Wm. B. Eerdmans Publishing Co.
255 Jefferson Ave. S.E., Grand Rapids, Michigan 49503 /
P.O. Box 163, Cambridge CB3 9PU U.K.

Published 1997
Paperback edition 1998
All rights reserved

Printed in the United States of America

02 01 00 99 98   7 6 5 4 3 2

Library of Congress Cataloging-in-Publication Data

Jones, Gareth Lloyd.
The bones of Joseph : from the ancient texts to the modern
church : studies in the Scriptures / by Gareth Lloyd Jones.
        p.   cm.
Includes bibliographical references.
ISBN 0-8028-4596-7 (pbk.: alk. paper)
1. Bible — Meditations. 2. Christian life — Meditations.
3. Christian life — Anglican authors. I. Title.
        BS491.5.J66   1997
        220.6 — dc21   97-8575
                    CIP

*Dedicated to the clergy and congregation of
St. David's Episcopal Church, Austin, Texas,
in gratitude for their friendship and hospitality*

Contents

Preface

THE FOLLOWING PAGES contain some of the fruits of almost a decade of lecturing and teaching in Britain and the United States. The individual chapters explore the meaning of selected passages from the Bible in an attempt to demonstrate the contemporary relevance of the biblical narrative. They started life as a series of lectures delivered to audiences of Anglican laypeople wishing to learn more about the Scriptures. In their written form they seek to provide the general reader with a blend of scholarship and spirituality. They presuppose no expertise in theology and no prior knowledge of the texts studied. The version of Scripture used throughout is the New English Bible (1970).

I am grateful to audiences and congregations in both the United Kingdom and the United States for their comments and suggestions made when these lectures were originally delivered. I owe a particular debt of gratitude to my colleague Dr. Margaret E. Thrall for reading the manuscript and making many significant improvements.

Gareth Lloyd Jones

The Bones of Joseph

Joseph said to his brothers, "I am dying; but God will not fail to come to your aid and take you from here to the land which he promised on oath to Abraham, Isaac and Jacob." He made the sons of Israel take an oath, saying, "When God thus comes to your aid, you must take my bones with you from here." So Joseph died at the age of one hundred and ten. He was embalmed and laid in a coffin in Egypt.

Genesis 50:24

Moses took the bones of Joseph with him, because Joseph had exacted an oath from the Israelites: "Some day," he said, "God will show his care for you, and then, as you go, you must take my bones with you."

Exodus 13:19

The bones of Joseph, which the Israelites had brought up from Egypt, were buried in Shechem, in the plot of land which Jacob had bought from the sons of Hamor for a hundred sheep.

Joshua 24:32

TRAVEL NORTH FROM JERUSALEM for about an hour and you will come to Nablus in the District of Samaria. On the opposite side of the valley to this bustling, restless city are two pilgrim shrines, Jacob's well and the tomb of Joseph. The tomb is an object of reverence for each of the three great monotheistic faiths: Judaism, Christianity, and Islam. This common veneration has meant that it has remained for centuries in pristine simplicity, disfigured by neither synagogue, church, nor mosque. A simple tomb with its traditional whitewashed dome stands within an enclosure. It is here, according to tradition, that Joseph was finally laid to rest over three thousand years ago.

He was buried originally in Egypt, but was disinterred by the fleeing slaves at the exodus and carefully carried for forty years through the desert until the Israelites reached Canaan. Only when the land was eventually conquered did he reach his last resting place. Given the circumstances, is it a credible story? At least two million people were involved in the exodus according to the record, and all escaped in one night. Would there have been time to look for Joseph at such short notice? Was his tomb not sealed or guarded? How easy was it to raid a pyramid? The rabbis circumvent the difficulty by claiming that Joseph's coffin was not placed in a burial chamber but lowered into the Nile. A washerwoman took Moses to the very spot four hundred years later and he hauled it out. Fortunately the factual details do not concern us here.

Clearly the reference to the burial of the bones in Shechem served some purpose in the early history of Israel. Perhaps the occasion was meant to mark Canaan out as the land of promise, and its possession by the Israelites as the fulfillment of God's pledge to Abraham that his descendants would have a home of their own. But for our purposes, the bones of Joseph will be regarded as a metaphor for tradition. The remains of the patriarch were carefully preserved, and when they were eventually buried in Canaan, they provided successive generations of Israelites with an important link with their past. Links with the past give meaning to the present and are vital for every historical religion. There must be roots, pedigree, and continuity. In other words, a historical religion has to take note of tradition; it is something that it cannot escape.

The Ubiquity of Tradition

Tradition is a word that has several shades of meaning, many of them linked to authority. The one that often comes to mind first is "custom." In this sense, tradition signifies those practices that belong to different Christian Churches; it refers to the way things are done. Even those Churches that came into being as a protest against certain conventions soon acquired traditions of their own. So there is an Anglican, a Presbyterian, a Methodist, and a Quaker tradition, to name but a few. These denominational traditions are reflected in architecture, government, ritual, liturgy, ministry, and the like, all of which represent patterns differing widely from Church to Church. In a given time and place they enriched the Church's life, and because they are hallowed by time, members often feel a deep emotional attachment to them. The danger is that they will be confused with what is essential, and as such become obstacles to the renewal of the Church's life. They can become rigid chains enslaving and stultifying, for they are often presented as tests of loyalty. Though a traditional custom may be defended on scriptural grounds, it is adhered to essentially because it is representative of the denomination concerned. In such matters the heart often rules the head — which is why religion can be so contentious.

But tradition is not to be identified only with denominational practice, it is also linked to "teaching" and "worship." Traditional teaching existed long before the New Testament came into being, in that the earliest Christian community possessed a traditional gospel and a traditional mode of worship. In the easily remembered rhythmical sentences of 1 Corinthians 15:1-8 we have a clue to the development of the creeds of later centuries:

> First and foremost, I handed on to you the facts which had been imparted to me: that Christ died for our sins, in accordance with the scriptures; that he was buried; that he was raised to life on the third day, according to the scriptures; and that he appeared to Cephas, and afterwards to the Twelve. Then he appeared to over five hundred of our brothers at once, most of whom are still alive, though some have died. Then he appeared to James, and afterwards to all the apostles. In the end he appeared even to me.

But before this text was written, the Church was already at work preaching the gospel. In other words, it had a tradition in the sense of a message to be handed on. The Bible is not our earliest teacher; behind it stands the community. The Church produced the Bible, not vice versa. The New Testament was written not to create faith, but to strengthen it and instruct people in the basis for it. In the beginning was the sermon, the oral tradition. Paul did not preach with a copy of the gospels open in front of him to give his words authority, as we do.

Whenever he was questioned by the inquisitive, he appealed to tradition, namely the testimony of Peter. The Bible is based on traditional teaching transmitted in an oral form.

The same is true of worship. Many churches regard the Eucharist as their main service and point to the evidence of Scripture. 1 Corinthians 11:23-26 is a favorite text:

> For I received from the Lord what I also delivered to you, that the Lord Jesus on the night when he was betrayed took bread, and when he had given thanks, he broke it, and said, "This is my body which is for you. Do this in remembrance of me." In the same way also he took the cup, after supper, saying, "This cup is the new covenant in my blood. Do this, as often as you drink it, in remembrance of me." For as often as you eat this bread and drink the cup, you proclaim the Lord's death until he comes.

But the Eucharist is not based primarily on the Bible, that is, on the written word, but on tradition. The Church was worshiping in this particular way long before the New Testament came into being. Until the sixteenth century, the authority for a particular form of worship was not the Bible, but usage. Hence the various Eucharistic "uses" linked to medieval cathedral foundations.

This brings us to what is perhaps the most significant meaning of tradition, namely, interpretation. In this sense tradition serves to elucidate the Scriptures by ensuring that we do not come to them cold, as it were. It enables us to read them in the light of what the Church has said about them. A. E. McGrath writes:

> Tradition is a willingness to read Scripture, taking into account the ways in which it has been read in the past. It is an awareness

of the communal dimension of Christian faith, which calls shallow individualism into question. There is more to the interpretation of Scripture than any one individual can discern. It is a willingness to give full weight to the views of those who have gone before us in the faith.[1]

It is noteworthy that in *Pilgrim's Progress* the first place Christian stops on his journey from the City of Destruction to the Heavenly City is the House of the Interpreter.

Tradition, therefore, is reflection upon Scripture. It is a particular way of reading and interpreting the Bible that the Church has recognized as authentic. While this specific approach first developed in response to the threat heretics posed to orthodox teaching in the early centuries, it was later reflected in the creeds. Doctrines that are only implied in the Bible were eventually made explicit in the dogmatic pronouncements of the Church, for example, the doctrine of the Trinity. In this sense tradition has been a bone of contention in Christian theology, mainly because it is linked to the question of authority, as the following examples will demonstrate.

Roman Catholicism has always laid great stress on tradition, by which it means the interpretation of the gospel as handed on by successive popes. The traditional teaching of the Church stands alongside Scripture as another source of revelation. This route led eventually to the doctrine of papal infallibility. Indeed, Pius IX said quite simply, "I am tradition." Since the Second Vatican Council there has been a renewal of interest in the Bible among Roman Catholics. But even so, the traditional interpretation is still authoritative for many significant issues. Protestants, on the other hand, have stressed the su-

1. A. E. McGrath, *Understanding Doctrine* (Grand Rapids: Zondervan, 1990), p. 25.

premacy of the Bible over tradition. The watchword of the Reformers was "Sola Scriptura" — by Scripture alone, the so-called Scripture principle. In an extreme form, this means that nothing can be taught or practiced unless it is explicitly authorized in the Bible. Today, however, most mainline Protestants acknowledge that tradition does have some positive role. Even conservative Baptist seminaries in America are beginning to teach church history.

Anglicans come somewhere between the two positions outlined above. That is, they try to hold in balance the various formative factors in theology, not allowing any one of them an overriding dominance. This standpoint can be traced to the sixteenth-century divine Richard Hooker, who advocated a multiform authority in matters theological. He opposed, on the one hand, the Roman Catholic claim for the supremacy of tradition, and on the other, the Protestant claim for a narrow and literalist view of the Bible. He accepted both in a modified form and added one other criterion — reason. In Hooker's synthesis, Scripture, tradition, and reason all had a place. Following in his footsteps, Anglicans have never put their trust in an infallible man or an infallible book. The Anglican concept of authority is not single-stranded, it is rather the threefold cord, not easily broken, of Bible, tradition, and reason. With reference to tradition Hooker says this: "For whatever we believe concerning salvation by Christ, although the Scripture be therein the ground of our belief, yet the authority of man is, if we mark it, the key which openeth the door of entrance into the knowledge of the Scripture. The Scripture could not teach us the things that are of God unless we did credit men who have taught us that the words of Scripture do signify those things."[2] For most of us, the first inkling of any

---

2. Richard Hooker, *Of the Laws of Ecclesiastical Polity,* quoted by E. J. Bicknell, *The Thirty-nine Articles,* 3rd ed. (London: Longmans, 1963), p. 129.

religious sense comes not from the Bible, but from the Sunday school or the enquirer's class, that is, "the authority of man," namely, tradition. The life of the Church illuminates and confirms the Bible. For Anglicans, the Bible is the basic authority, but standing alongside it to interpret it is the Church. Bible and Church go hand in hand.

To sum up: Interpretation is always conditioned by the tradition in which the reader stands. No Christian can go to the Scriptures free from the influence of tradition; a person can never clear his or her mind of the received interpretation. But even if one could, no sensible person would want to do so. On the contrary, he or she would be only too glad to have his or her own mind enlightened by the corporate mind of the Church and to be directed by its communal wisdom. Like Christian, the person would call first at the House of the Interpreter.

Attitudes to Tradition

The biblical account of what happened to the bones of Joseph suggests two possible reactions to tradition: the revolutionary and the radical. The difference between these two reactions was spelled out by Bishop John Robinson at the height of the "honest to God" debate in the sixties.[3] His distinction forms the basis of the following remarks.

On their way from Egypt to Canaan, the Israelites tried more than once, metaphorically speaking, to discard the bones of Joseph. Several times they turned their backs on their tradition. They complained that Moses had tricked them by bringing them into the desert where they faced certain death, and they begged to be allowed to return to Egypt. When this request

3. See John Robinson, *The New Reformation?* (London: SCM, 1965).

failed, they decided to go their own way by substituting a golden calf for Jehovah. Later, after they settled in Canaan, paganism seemed to be a far more attractive option than the traditional religion of Sinai. The same rejection of tradition is recorded in the New Testament. Paul writes thus to the Galatians:

> I am astonished to find you turning so quickly away from him who called you by grace, and following a different gospel. Not that it is in fact another gospel; only there are persons who unsettle your minds by trying to distort the gospel of Christ. But if anyone, if we ourselves or an angel from heaven, should preach a gospel at variance with the gospel we preached to you, he shall be held outcast. (1:6-8)

In both politics and religion this negative response to tradition may be regarded as that of the revolutionary, who, in Robinson's words, is an "outsider to the structure he would see collapse."[4] The one who calls for revolution deliberately separates himself or herself from the tradition, because for such a person it is irreformable; orthodoxy enslaves. In the interests of freedom, the entire structure has to be overthrown, and such action may well involve ruthlessness. The revolutionary is quite content to be without theological roots, preferring not to be hassled by history.

The attitude of the radical is quite different. Undoubtedly the prophets of Israel venerated the bones of Joseph, in that they were keenly aware of the importance of traditional teaching. Much of their own preaching was based on the Law of

4. John Robinson, "On Being a Radical," *The Listener* (21 Feb. 1963), quoted by D. L. Edwards in J. A. T. Robinson and D. L. Edwards, *The Honest to God Debate* (London: SCM, 1963), p. 28.

Moses. But although they criticized their contemporaries' understanding of that ancient teaching, they were not revolutionaries, but radicals. As the derivation of the word implies, the radical goes to the root of his or her own tradition and seeks to discover its purpose. The radical stands within it and never steps outside it. The radical pronounces doom, but still weeps over his or her people. The radical has respect for the basic beliefs of his or her faith and seeks to provide the correct interpretation of them. In this sense, the radical is close to the fundamentalist. "Both are concerned to go to the essentials. The difference is that the fundamentalist sees these in inorganic terms, as foundations; the radical in organic terms, as roots. And digging around foundations and digging around roots can have very different consequences. Disturb the foundations and the whole building may collapse. That is why the security of the fundamentalist is notoriously brittle. He dare not question too much, lest everything slip. The courage of the radical has a much more supple strength."[5]

There is all the difference in the world between a respect for tradition and a doctrine of no change. They are, in fact, incompatible, because the tradition itself has been in a constant state of change. The attempt to freeze it would be to deny an important element in it. Tradition has always been something alive. To be alive is to be growing, and to be growing is to be changing. That is one of the differences between foundations and roots. As Canon Ian Dunlop has pointed out, "Tradition must not be thought of as some mediaeval castle into which we retreat and pull up the drawbridge and from which we hurl slogans at those who disagree with us. It should be something organic and growing, with a digestive system which enables it

5. J. A. T. Robinson, "Not Radical Enough?" *The Christian Century* (12 Nov. 1969): p. 1446.

to take on board new insights and retain what is useful of the old."[6] Tradition includes the concept of development. A nostalgic preoccupation with the old may well indicate that the faith is being used as an escape from contemporary life; that religion is being regarded as a bolt-hole to shield us from having to face reality. Tradition must not become preferable to truth. If it does, there can never be any development of doctrine or ethics in the light of new knowledge.

The Value of Tradition

Given the ubiquity and significance of tradition within the Christian faith, what is its abiding value? Why should it be preserved? One reason is that it serves to unite its adherents. The bones of Joseph, once they had been finally buried in Canaan, must have served as a focal point for the Israelites. His tomb shared the characteristics of all great shrines — it became a center that attracted pilgrims from all corners of the country, bringing them together with the shared aim of venerating the memory of their ancestor. The simple, whitewashed patriarchal grave made all who journeyed to it conscious of their common heritage.

In the last two decades, the major Christian bodies have experienced a growing awareness of their common calling. This period is distinguished from the past by the Churches' new readiness to listen to one another and to explore together the essence of Christianity. This does not imply abandonment of truth for the sake of peace. Rather, it is an attempt to see whether the differing insights of the various parties may not

6. Ian Dunlop, "Thinking it Out, 'Tradition v. Trend,'" *Church Times* (22 Jan. 1988).

be as incompatible as in the heat of controversy they may seem to be. It is an attempt to see whether there may not be some deeper truth behind our present positions, to see where unity and truth may indeed meet together. For example, in recent years Professor Hans Küng has called for a renewed concentration on "Jesus himself and his message." This appeal sounds commonplace to Protestants, but for many Roman Catholics, reared on a diet of ecclesiology with its emphasis on the teaching of the Church rather than on the contents of the Scriptures, it may be new and challenging. But in fact, Küng is doing no more than going back to the original tradition. The effect of such action is to discover common ground shared by other Christians. In other words, the center remains the same even though the edges and the ends are open and expanding.

But tradition not only unites, it guards. Assuming that we are justified in regarding the bones of Joseph as a metaphor for tradition, they must have been a powerful symbol in ancient Israel. They reminded pilgrims of the glorious past of their people: the exodus, the covenant on Sinai, the wanderings through the desert, and the gift of land. The Old Testament authors never cease to insist that this ancient tradition, represented by the tomb at Shechem, be remembered. Those who neglect it are condemned unsparingly, as Psalm 78 makes plain. In this lengthy pslam the author records the faithlessness of Israel in several verses. Though saved by God, the Israelites forgot all that he had done (v. 11); they had no faith in his wonderful acts (v. 32); they were not loyal to him in their hearts (v. 37); they did not remember his prowess (v. 42). We have here a powerful indictment of the people's rejection of tradition. In the psalmist's view, history justifies such censure, for Israel succumbed to paganism, which in turn brought punishment. The loss of tradition made Israel vulnerable to the pernicious influence of idolatry. The psalm shows what happens when the community tries to live without reference to a tradition, without a corporate memory, without a clear identity. Amnesia extracts a severe penalty.

Does not this psalm point also to the truism that only the appreciation of tradition enables us to put a critical distance between ourselves and every new religious ideology? Tradition exists to ensure that we are not at the mercy of some bright spark with a new idea. There must be a standard by which we can identify legitimate development; there must be some thread of continuity. A growing Church must be recognizably the same Church. Tradition acts as a bulwark against individualism and an unrestrained enthusiasm in theological matters. Scripture needs tradition to guard it against private interpretations of biblical texts, for almost anything can be read into the Bible. Control has to be exercised by the mind of the Church expressed in traditional interpretation.

Finally, tradition guides. Soon after I was ordained, I was invited to a country parish on the island of Anglesey off the Welsh coast to preach at Evensong. I traveled the narrow lanes confidently until I came to a crossroads. Since there was no signpost and I was unsure of the way, I was presented with three possible routes by which to beat the deadline to my appointment. As I pondered which way to go, a farmer approached on his bicycle. Recognizing my difficulty, he dismounted and asked me what I considered at the time was a meaningless question: "Where have you come from?" He clearly thought that he would find it easier to help me find my way forward if he knew something about the route I had already taken.

Perhaps there is a moral in that story when we consider the role of tradition as a guide. A French saying puts the concept in a nutshell: "Step back in order to jump further." Advance may often begin by retracing our steps. The psalmist makes this point clearly:

> He laid on Jacob a solemn charge
> and established a law in Israel,
> which he commanded our fathers
> to teach their sons,
> that it might be known to a future generation,
> to children yet unborn,
> and these would repeat it to their sons in turn.
> He charged them to put their trust in God,
> to hold his great acts ever in mind. (Ps. 78:5-7)

The tradition is recited so that the people should set their hope on God. In other words, there can be no expectations if there are no memories. Our capacity to hope is precisely correlated with our ability to remember. Memory puts an important past behind the present, for in the Bible the great acts of God in the past are taken as models of what he will do in the future. As Israel remembers that God divided the sea to save its ancestors, so it hopes that he will once more deliver his people when they call on him. The tradition is preserved to show that the future is not closed and fated. It challenges complacency. As Henri Nouwen points out, great Christian reformers down the ages — Benedict in the sixth century, Francis in the twelfth, Luther in the sixteenth, Wesley in the eighteenth, and Pope John XXIII in the twentieth — have adopted the same method: they have challenged the value system of their own age by recalling their contemporaries to the basic gospel message.[7] Every period of renewal in the history of the Church has been

7. Henri Nouwen, *The Living Reminder* (New York: Seabury, 1977), pp. 63ff.

dominated by a return to the original tradition whence the inspiration first came. The English Reformation, of which many of us are heirs, was as much an appeal to the past as a venture into the future. The same could surely be said of the religion of the Israelites as they crossed the Sinai desert, Egypt behind them, Canaan ahead of them, carrying with them the bones of Joseph.

A Trick That Worked

In course of time Joseph died, he and all his brothers and that whole generation. Now the Israelites were fruitful and prolific; they increased in numbers and became very powerful, so that the country was overrun by them. Then a new king ascended the throne of Egypt, one who knew nothing of Joseph. He said to his people, "These Israelites have become too many and too strong for us. We must take precautions to see that they do not increase any further; or we shall find that, if war breaks out, they will join the enemy and fight against us, and they will become masters of the country." So they were made to work in gangs with officers set over them, to break their spirit with heavy labour. This is how Pharaoh's store cities, Pithom and Rameses, were built. But the more harshly they were treated, the more their numbers increased beyond all bounds, until the Egyptians came to loathe the sight of them. So they treated their Israelite slaves with ruthless severity, and made life bitter for them with cruel servitude, setting them to work on clay and brick-making, and all sorts of work in the fields. In short they made ruthless use of them as slaves in every kind of hard labour.

Then the king of Egypt spoke to the Hebrew midwives, whose names were Shiphrah and Puah. "When you are attending the Hebrew women in childbirth," he told them, "watch as the child is delivered and if it is a boy, kill him; if it is a girl, let her live." But they were God-fearing women. They did not do what the king of Egypt had told them to do, but let the boys live. They told Pharaoh that Hebrew women were not like Egyptian women. When they were in labour they gave birth before the midwife could get to them. So God made the midwives prosper, and the people increased in numbers and in strength. God gave the midwives homes and families of their own, because they feared him. Pharaoh then ordered all his people to throw every new-born Hebrew boy into the Nile, but to let the girls live.

A descendant of Levi married a Levite woman who conceived and bore a son. When she saw what a fine child he was, she hid him for three months, but she could conceal him no longer. So she got a rush basket for him, made it watertight with clay and tar, laid him in it, and put it among the reeds by the bank of the Nile. The child's sister took her stand at a distance to see what would happen to him. Pharaoh's daughter came down to bathe in the river, while her ladies-in-waiting walked along the bank. She noticed the basket among the reeds and sent her slave-girl for it. She took it from her and when she opened it, she saw the child. It was crying, and she was filled with pity for it. "Why," she said, "it is a little Hebrew boy." Thereupon the sister said to Pharaoh's daughter, "Shall I go and fetch one of the Hebrew women as a wet-nurse to suckle the child for you?" Pharaoh's daughter told her to go; so the girl went and called the baby's mother. Then Pharaoh's daughter said to her, "Here is the child, suckle him for me, and I will pay you for it myself." So the woman took the child and suckled him. When the child was old enough, she brought him

to Pharaoh's daughter, who adopted him and called him Moses,
"because," she said, "I drew him out of the water."

Exodus 1:6–2:10

Each of the great monotheistic religions has at least three ways of expressing and preserving its beliefs: hymns, creeds, and stories. An ancient and well-tried method of proclaiming a faith and making it memorable is to put it to music. The basic doctrines of Christianity are "preserved unforgotten" in our hymns. This is perhaps the most popular form of proclamation, for theology at least sounds easier if it rhymes. Though now associated with hymnbooks, the Christian practice of expressing religious belief in verse goes back to New Testament times. On two occasions (Phil. 2:6-11; Col. 1:15-20) Paul speaks of the nature of Christ in what seems to be meter. Some bibles even print the relevant verses as poetry. Whether Paul composed these poems himself or was quoting another writer is not clear. If he was the author, by using hymns to make theological statements he was simply following the tradition of the synagogue. For centuries his forefathers had made doctrinal statements in the Psalter, a book described as "Israel's creed, sung but not signed."

The second form of expression is the creed proper, as in the Apostles' Creed or the Nicene Creed, both of which are recited regularly in Anglican services. The creed is much more complex than the hymn — witness the Athanasian Creed, which, according to the Book of Common Prayer of 1662, is to be said at Morning Prayer fourteen times a year, including Christmas Day, Easter Sunday, and Pentecost. But though these creeds reflect the doctrinal controversies of the early Church, the principle behind their formulation can be traced to the New Testament. A concise statement of belief such as "Jesus is Lord"

18

(Rom. 10:9) was a feature of Christian worship from the beginning. This again was a practice taken over from Judaism, for the essence of an ancient Israelite creed may be found in Deuteronomy 26:5-9 and Joshua 24:2-13.

But here I want to concentrate on the third, and perhaps the most significant, method of propagating religious faith, namely story. In all religions stories are used to convey theological truth, to expound the creed. In Christianity the infancy and resurrection narratives illustrate and explain, in a vivid and memorable form, key doctrinal statements. The same is true of Judaism. The first fourteen chapters of the Book of Exodus, for example, expand in story form on the claim made time and again in the Hebrew Scriptures that God liberated his people from bondage in Egypt. In the hands of the storyteller, the pivotal statement with which the Ten Commandments opens, "I am the Lord your God who brought you out of Egypt, out of the land of slavery" (Exod. 20:2), becomes an exciting yarn.

As we consider the Bible's introduction to the story of Israel's freedom from bondage, we should note some of the stylistic features and literary devices of the narrative. It is important that we recognize the skill of the teller of tales, who sometimes "touches the hem of genius." When the tale was first told, the perceptive listener would have recognized key phrases and recurring words employed deliberately to send out signals and make connections. The Israelites would have enjoyed the irony that pervades the account. If the modern reader does not appreciate these literary techniques, the story loses much of its impact.

In seeking to appreciate the author's intention, it must be remembered that while the event of liberation is central to the first half of the book (chs. 1–18), the historical minutiae are peripheral. Much of the detail is religious or didactic; in other words, its purpose is theological and educational. The author embroiders the narrative in order to instruct his readers in the tenets of Israelite religion. He does not simply provide an unadorned account of the flight from Egypt, but presents the event as it was explored and reflected upon from the perspective of faith, an activity that went on orally for centuries before the stories were committed to writing. Because history and faith are inseparably interwoven, the true significance of the book is not to be sought in the factual details but in the significance of what happened, as that is perceived long after the event. Biblical history discovers meaning more than it reproduces facts. It contains interpretation, which gives an ordinary event a deeper or transcendent significance. It has been suggested that biblical narrative should be regarded as a portrait, not as a photograph. While the cameraman records objects in an unselective and unbiased manner, the artist chooses what he wants to emphasize. While the photographer records the superficial or external aspects, the painter sees in the physical form the reality that lies behind it.

The Bible was not written, primarily, to describe events as they happened, but to interpret them after they had happened. The Gospels, for instance, are not now regarded as biographies of Jesus, because it is recognized that their contents are influenced by faith in the risen Christ. The authors were driven to write not only because of their interest in the historical Jesus but because of their belief that he was the Son of God. This has led to a consensus among biblical scholars that the Bible is to be read more as theology than history, that it consists essentially of theological interpretation and is therefore not the best guide for historical reconstruction. One cannot presume upon its factual reliability. In any case, there are deeper truths than a quest for historicity would uncover. It is to these truths, as they appear in the account of the preparations made for Israel's deliverance from slavery in Egypt, that we now turn.

20

A Cruel King

The basic concept behind the Exodus story is that of liberation from bondage, which in theological terms is described as redemption, deliverance, and salvation. The account begins with a dramatic portrayal of the need for liberation by describing the pharaoh's reign of terror and his persecution of the Israelites. This king, who is not named, begins a new dynasty in Egypt and knows nothing of the invaluable service rendered by Joseph to one of his predecessors when he saved the country from famine. As he reviews the political situation, he becomes suspicious of a nonintegrated group of immigrants living in the far north of the country and is convinced that its size constitutes a threat to the stability of the realm. He may have had good reason to fear the Israelites, for they were increasing rapidly, as the biblical record demonstrates. In the opening verses of Exodus we move swiftly from the twelve sons of Jacob to seventy people and then to a vast throng. In 1:7 five verbs are used to stress the vitality of the Israelites and their extraordinary proliferation. We are told that they "were fruitful and prolific; they increased in numbers and became very powerful, so that the country was overrun by them."

Since economy is the hallmark of Hebrew style, this deliberate repetition is meant to convey a message that the initiated will easily grasp. By using the language of growth the author recalls two key texts in the Book of Genesis. The first is Genesis 1:28, where the Creator blesses the first humans by saying to them, "Be fruitful and increase, fill the earth and subdue it." The second is God's intention, mentioned in Genesis 18:18, of making Abraham into "a great and powerful nation." Both of these texts are reflected in the opening verses of Exodus. Thus the birth of the Israelite nation is linked to the birth of the world, and its strength marks the beginning of the fulfillment of the promise of progeny made to Abraham. The specific vocabulary used here to describe the Israelites is meant to demonstrate that the divine purpose was gradually being worked out even under an oppressive regime. It is an indirect but effective way of saying that God, though not yet mentioned in the text, is with his people.

While the pharaoh was oblivious to the theological implications of this demographic explosion, he was fully aware of the political threat that it carried. He realized that he would soon be unable to control such incredible expansion and prevent the Israelites from joining his enemies in the event of an invasion (Exod. 1:10). The king responded to the perceived danger in an entirely predictable fashion — by tightening the screws. He proceeded to allay his fears by taking the necessary "precautions," or as other translations render this verse, he proposed to "deal wisely" with the Israelites. He rapidly implemented new policies, which included severely repressive measures, to ensure that they did not "increase any further." An experienced oppressor, he sought to solve the problem of proliferation and banish the threat of insurrection by enacting three laws designed to cripple the Israelites, an enterprise in which he enlisted the help of the whole population (Exod. 1:9). Since his subjects shared his anxiety and had come "to loathe the sight of" the Israelites (Exod. 1:12), they willingly participated in any plan to curb the expansion.

The first law would ensure that the hapless immigrants remained politically insignificant by engaging them in forced labor under Egyptian taskmasters. "They were made to work in gangs with officers set over them, to break their spirit with heavy labour" (Exod. 1:11). Egyptians were appointed to supervise the laborers as they built the pharaoh's store cities and to prevent them from acquiring any political standing. Israelites were not eligible to act as foremen. They were allowed no voice or vote in their own affairs. Trade unions were prohibited. The immigrants from Canaan, welcomed by an earlier pharaoh, had become slaves; they were compelled to work for the state.

Though slavery has ceased to exist, at least in theory, the picture painted in Exodus 1:11 is by no means unfamiliar three thousand years later. Do we not see here one of the principles of apartheid, which, until recently, ensured that black South Africans remained disenfranchised? Do we not see here the reason why the "Solidarity" movement took root in the Polish shipyards a little more than a decade ago? Do we not see here one of the main causes of the nationalist unrest now prevalent in what was once the Soviet Union? The need for liberation is most keenly felt when any nation or ethnic group is regarded by a dominant power as being politically insignificant.

The purpose of the second law was to keep the Israelites in a perpetual state of exhaustion and intellectual stagnation. The language of despair and oppression is prominent throughout the first chapter of Exodus and reappears in the fifth. The gang-foremen, the heavy labor, the building projects, the harsh treatment, the cruel servitude "made life bitter" for the Israelites (Exod. 2:13-14). The fivefold repetition of the Hebrew word translated "service" or "labour" in these two verses indicates the severity of life for the internees and balances the five verbs used in verse 7 to indicate the increase in the population. In the brickworks the pharaoh adds to their misery by refusing to provide the material for making bricks; the slaves must collect their own straw in the lunch hour "but produce the same tally of bricks as before" (Exod. 5:8).

Why such a callous regime? It seems that the king was deliberately curtailing the Israelites' leisure time in order to ensure their subservience and complicity. This is the rationale of the concentration camp, where those suspected of crimes against the state are sentenced to harsh manual labor from dawn to dusk. The regime assures that the inmates have no time for themselves. And this is crucial, for people without leisure are deprived of the opportunity to further their education, to exchange ideas, to share experiences, and to plan any kind of resistance. The vast majority will cause no trouble because they are too exhausted to care. They will be amenable and docile because they lack the energy to think or plan, let alone fight. Pharaoh's Egypt provides us with a wholly contemporary picture.

However, despite the pharaoh's best-laid plans, the opposite of what he expected occurs: the Israelite population continues to grow. "The more harshly they were treated, the more their numbers increased beyond all bounds" (Exod. 1:12). The first two solutions to the problem of the immigrants are unsuccessful. Severe repression and exploitation fail to lessen the birthrate or to minimize the threat of insurrection. So in desperation the king devises a new plan that involves more than hard labor or brutal overseers. He gives the order to kill. He opts for genocide, believing that he will achieve his aim by taking the girls into his harem and destroying the boys. He starts by enlisting the help of two midwives as his special agents. But they disobey his command and allow the boys to live. Finally, his plans thwarted once more, the king turns again to his people and orders the whole population to cooperate. He instructs them to "throw every new-born Hebrew boy into the Nile, but to let the girls live" (Exod. 1:22).

The motives behind such barbarism are by no means clear. Why would a ruler wish to destroy his own labor supply? It has been suggested that he acted as he did because he was paranoid. Referring to the slaughter of the innocents, Everett Fox makes a pertinent comparison: "The story does not describe a rational fear, but paranoia — paralleling the situation in Nazi Germany of the late 1930s and 1940s, where Jews were blamed for various economic and political catastrophes not of their own making and were eliminated from a society that could have used their resources and manpower."[1] The parallel extends further. Just as the pharaoh needed the active cooperation of the Egyptians if he was to succeed, so the Nazis had to persuade the German nation that the only way to deal with Jews was to eliminate them. Hitler's "final solution" of the Jewish problem followed the same course as that of the Egyptian despot, except that under the Nazis the girls were murdered as well.

Such were the laws of a cruel king. They were included in the story in order to underline the Israelites' need for deliverance. They were enacted because the pharaoh was afraid of his slaves. Initially, because of the introduction of forced labor, his fear may have been justified. A brickworks may be profitable for the owner, but for those compelled to work there it is a place of misery and hopelessness. The prevailing mood among the disadvantaged is one of despair, and despair invariably breeds enmity, which often erupts into open conflict. This in turn strikes fear into the heart of the oppressor, who reacts by making life even more difficult. The same spiral of despair, enmity, fear, and violence lies at the heart of much of the political instability in the modern world. The peoples of South Africa, Latin America, and Eastern Europe have been only too well aware of it for much of this century. No absolute ruler can afford to stop looking over his shoulder; like the pharaoh, he inevitably becomes paranoid. Hitler, Stalin, and Ceaucescu, to name but three, serve as contemporary examples.

It would be difficult to imagine laws more ideally suited to destroy a nation than these, for they begin with apartheid and end with genocide. But they prove to be totally ineffective. Why?

---

1. Everett Fox, *Now These Are the Names: A New English Rendition of the Book of Exodus* (New York: Schocken Books, 1986), p. 15.

Because the two people whom the pharaoh chose to implement his plan defied him. Commanded to kill all Israelite boys at birth, the midwives refused to do so. The reason given for their disobedience, which entailed considerable risk, is that they were "God-fearing women" (Exod. 1:17). To "fear God" does not mean being afraid of divine punishment. Rather it implies conduct based on ethical principles and in harmony with the will of God. The midwives refused to kill because they had a respect for life. For them, "fearing God" did not involve prayers and sacrifices but the saving of innocent people. When their disregard for the royal injunction was noticed, they were summoned back to the palace to explain their disobedience. Although the pharaoh's response is not recorded, it must be assumed that he believed them when they claimed that they could not carry out his policy because the Hebrew women did not need the assistance of a midwife; unlike the Egyptians they gave birth very easily. Everything was over before help arrived. Because of their positive response to the divine will, the midwives prospered and the people continued to increase in numbers.

From the standpoint of the narrator several features of this story are worthy of note. The first is the implausibility of some of the factual details. According to the biblical record, over six hundred thousand "men in the prime of life" came out of Egypt during the Exodus. Assuming that each one had a wife, well over a million Israelites lived in captivity. But there were only two midwives. Assisting at all the deliveries would have been an impossible task. The difficulty is compounded if, as is suggested, the two midwives attended Egyptian women as well. Perhaps the pharaoh entrusted his genocidal policy to elected representatives of a large group of midwives, but this in not what the text says. Futhermore it is highly unlikely that Hebrew midwives would have had audiences with the pharaoh himself. Bearing in mind the status of women in the ancient world, it is far more probable that they were summoned to speak to a minor official. But such improbabilities do not worry the narrator. He is concerned only with telling a good story that will grip his readers. A tale about two midwives hoodwinking a king face to face, however implausible, is far more compelling and entertaining than a bald account of the proclamation of a royal decree.

In the original Hebrew the nationality of the midwives is ambiguous. Though the English text says that "the king of Egypt spoke to the Hebrew midwives" (Exod. 1:15), it is not clear whether this refers to Hebrew women who acted as midwives to both the Israelites and the Egyptians or to Egyptian women who served among the Israelites. This ambiguity has led commentators to offer two readings of the story, both heavy with irony. If the women were Israelites, the pharaoh's choice of them to carry out his plans is yet another example of the stupidity of the god-king who had resolved only a few verses previously to "take precautions" to curb the increase of the immigrants. Surrounded though he is by advisers and wise men, the mighty monarch is duped by two insignificant midwives. The irony would appeal to the audience. Furthermore, if they were Israelites, the women must be counted alongside Moses as deliverers of their own people. In a patriarchal society like ancient Israel, such a claim is by no means insignificant. But if the midwives were Egyptians, then they must be reckoned as the first "righteous gentiles," those non-Jews who put their own lives at risk to save Jewish friends and neighbors from murderous mobs. If they were Egyptians, it must be recognized that their fear of God, their sense of right and wrong and their readiness to act on it, transcended their fear of the king, who was considered divine by his subjects. The pharaoh had among his people those who followed the dictates of conscience rather than the decrees of the state. Here too the irony of the situation would appeal to the audience.

Perhaps the most significant detail about the two midwives is that they are named, for naming turns the spotlight on them in no uncertain terms.[2] They appear in a story that has a cast of millions. But in the first two chapters of Exodus only the hero and his wife, son, and father-in-law are given names. Moses' parents and sister are mentioned but not named; likewise the pharaoh, his daughter, and her ladies-in-waiting are mentioned but not named. All these play a crucial part in the story but they are not identified, at least not immediately, because they are secondary characters. Their lack of identification helps the reader to focus on the hero and on his name. Shiphrah and Puah, however, are given names at once, which suggests that they were recognized by the narrator as having a key role in the eventual liberation of the Israelites.

But however laudable the action of the midwives, one element in their story has perplexed Christian commentators from the fourth century onwards, namely God's readiness to reward their deception. In the text the reference to their alleged inability to reach the Hebrew women in time to deliver their children is followed immediately by the words: "So God made the midwives prosper" (Exod. 1:20). They were given homes and families of their own. Did this divine recompense imply that deceit, under certain circumstances, was justifiable? Saint Augustine was the first to treat the passage in any detail, and he concluded that the midwives were rewarded not for telling lies, but for assisting the Israelites; in his view, lying is never justified. Gregory the Great also argued that their duplicity was reprehensible and that, although they were rewarded, God's displeasure with the two women was revealed in the nature of the reward. Their recompense was earthly rather than heavenly

---

2. This point is well made by Trevor Dennis, *Sarah Laughed: Women's Voices in the Old Testament* (London: SPCK, 1994), pp. 88f.

because they had been deceitful. Martin Luther, on the other hand, tended to be more lenient. He justified their lying because the intention was laudable; their aim was to aid rather than injure. Claus Westermann also finds deceit justifiable in certain circumstances when he says, in the context of Abraham passing Sarah off as his sister to the Egyptians in order to save his own skin (Gen. 12:10-20): "The ruse is the only weapon left for the powerless given over to the mighty."[3] The liberation from bondage begins with a trick.

A Crucial Family

The continuation of the story in chapter two does not immediately strike one as logical. With the threat of genocide hanging over them, it would not be surprising if the Israelites had called a general strike or planned a rebellion. They might have organized clandestine meetings to prepare for revolution by drawing up a manifesto. But they do none of these things. The narrative focuses not on a national upheaval, but on the crisis facing a particular family. The central character is not a freedom fighter who calls on his compatriots to resist, but a baby hidden in the rushes on the bank of the Nile. Although, as becomes apparent, the child already has an older brother and sister, he is introduced as if he were the firstborn, because the spotlight is going to be on him. Moses is elevated at the expense of his older siblings. The tale is divided into three parts: the disposal of the child in the river, the discovery of the basket by the princess, and the adoption of the boy into the royal family. His birth is mentioned only in passing; no special significance is

3. Claus Westermann, *Genesis 12–36: A Commentary* (SPCK: London 1986), p. 164.

attached to it. There is no annunciation, there are no miracles, and nothing marks the spot where he was born. All that is conveyed is the sense of danger surrounding the incident.

Following on from the last phrase in chapter one, "let the girls live," the first half of the second chapter is dominated by women: after the child's conception his father plays no part in the proceedings. The story revolves around Moses' real mother, his sister, and the princess with her companions. Those whom the pharaoh allowed to survive will turn out to be the very ones who undermine his policy of genocide. The child is born of parents from the tribe of Levi, the third of Jacob's twelve sons. Though listed as one of the tribes of Israel, Levi was different from the rest in that it owned no land. Its members earned their living by performing sacral functions for the other tribes. The Levites consecrated themselves as priests in the service of God. The fact that Moses was numbered among them establishes his credentials and indicates something special about his descent. This detail is particularly significant on account of his Egyptian upbringing and in view of the priestly duties he is to perform later.

When his mother "saw what a fine child he was, she hid him for three months" from those who were carrying out the pharaoh's orders to kill. Some commentators claim that this is a reference to the boy's robustness rather than his beauty. It would have been a tragedy to lose even a puny weakling to the king's death squads, how much more a child that was healthy and unlikely to succumb to infant diseases. But whatever the correct interpretation, the original Hebrew contains a phrase that again sends out a coded message in that it reflects the language of the creation story. Literally translated, Exodus 2:2 reads as: "and she saw him, that he was good, and she hid him for three months." The phrase "that he was good" is identical with the one used throughout the first chapter of Genesis to describe God's pleasure at each stage of creation: "and God saw that it [he] was good." (In Hebrew there is no neuter, only masculine and feminine.) As the birth of the nation was given added significance by linking the proliferation of the immigrants verbally to the creation of the world, so the birth of Moses is placed within the context of God's creative work.

The infancy narrative provides the storyteller with yet another opportunity to highlight the religious significance of Moses. In order to conceal him among the reeds, his mother placed him in "a rush basket," literally "an ark of papyrus," a material that floats. The only other appearance in the Bible of the Hebrew word used here for "basket" or "ark" is in the story of Noah (Gen. 6–9), which suggests that the author is drawing a parallel between Moses and the hero of the Flood. Both were saved by God from drowning because they were destined to become deliverers of their people; Noah built an ark to save humanity, Moses led Israel out of captivity. For both the waters of destruction became the waters of liberation. Trevor Dennis explains the significance of the link between the infancy of Moses and the story of the Flood by saying that the narrator "is indicating the momentous character of the events. He is, in effect, making the extraordinary claims that with the birth of Moses a new era in the history of the world has dawned, and that through him, as through Noah, God will bring about a dramatic act of salvation, and rescue his purposes from the dark waters of violence."[4] The audience is expected to make significant comparisons.

The sister who appears out of nowhere is presumably the Miriam mentioned in later chapters. She watches the floating basket from the bank and thereby reduces the threat posed to her infant brother by exposure to the elements. But she plays

4. Dennis, p. 98.

31

an even more important role in the tale. Her introduction at this point has been recognized by commentators as a literary device of the narrator. She serves to link the introduction with the rest of the story because she stands between the hiding and the finding of the boy. She acts as a mediator between the slave and the princess, the child's natural mother and his adoptive mother, by bringing them together. It is her initiative that will shape the destiny of Moses.

The third female figure is the pharaoh's daughter, who comes to bathe in the river with her maidservants. The fact that she is an Egyptian princess is an important detail in that Moses is saved by someone from within the enemy camp and brought up in the palace of the one who tried to kill him, thus increasing the irony of the situation. When the basket is found and opened, the king's daughter comes face to face with an Israelite child, probably for the first time in her life. She knows that he is to be regarded as an enemy of the state, even in his cradle, but "she was filled with pity" for him. His tears pierce her heart. She sees among the rushes not a potential enemy, but a human being. She has no right to feel compassion; the law of the land, promulgated by her own father, is quite explicit. But her maternal instinct persuades her otherwise. It dictates her feelings and prevents her from appreciating the reasons of state. She turns out to be firmly pro-life when she knowingly ignores her father's edict. Her compassion transcends the distinctions of rank and nationality. If the midwives were Israelites, then the princess is the first "righteous gentile."

While the princess is contemplating her discovery, the child's sister reappears and makes a suggestion that will alleviate the boy's plight. She assumes that the princess will want to adopt the infant and offers to find her a nurse from among the Israelites. The offer is accepted, with the result that Moses' own mother is brought into the palace to care for him until he is weaned, which usually took place about three years after birth. She is even promised payment for doing so. The child is then legally adopted, receives an Egyptian name, and becomes part of the royal household. The princess was responsible for his upbringing and apparently did a commendable job. Stephen, in his speech in Acts 7:23, reflects an ancient Jewish tradition when he refers to Moses as one who "was trained in all the wisdom of the Egyptians, a powerful speaker and a man of action." According to the same source he spent forty years at the pharaoh's court before he left to become a shepherd in the land of Midian. But while his adoptive mother provided his education, it was his natural mother who taught him patience, love, and fortitude. It was at her knee that he learned to hate injustice and cruelty. It was because of her influence that he appears later as one who sides with right against might.

Because Moses survives against all odds, the account of his birth and adoption carries a strong hint that this child will one day be important. But is the story fancy or fact? At least two considerations militate against accepting it as a factual biography. The first is the recognition that elements in it are themes that are found in several other birth stories. Many legendary heroes in the ancient world, of whom a list of thirty-five has been compiled, share the characteristics of Moses' remarkable childhood. One of the most striking examples is that of Sargon, who ruled Akkad in Mesopotamia at about 2300 BC. Referring to his own pedigree, Sargon writes in his autobiography of how he was born, abandoned, found, and adopted before the goddess Ishtar made him king:

I am Sargon, the mighty king, the king of Akkad.
My mother was a changeling; I never knew my father.
My city is Azupiranu, situated on the banks of the Euphrates.
My changeling mother conceived me and bore me in secret.

She laid me in a basket of rushes, sealed it with asphalt,
And cast me on the river which did not rise over me.
The river bore me to Akki, the drawer of water.
He lifted me out as he dipped his bucket.
He took me as a son and reared me; he made me his
  gardener.
When I was a gardener Ishtar gave me her love,
And for fifty years I exercised kingship.

Despite some differences, there are obvious parallels between this and the Exodus account. The story of Sargon, which
is a thousand years older than that of Moses, would have been
well known in the ancient world, as would many others like
it. The biblical author could well have used it when he came
to write about Moses.

The second consideration is linked to the universal ten-
dency to magnify the famous by scrutinizing their origins and
noting any extraordinary circumstances in their early life. As
soon as people make their mark in the world, the search for
their origins and for portents of their greatness starts. If Jesus
of Nazareth had not been raised from the dead, the infancy
stories would not have been written and Bethlehem would not
be the tourist attraction it is today. If Abraham Lincoln had
not gone to the White House, we would never have heard of
the log cabin. If Saint David had not become such an important symbol of independence for the medieval Welsh church,
his biographer would not have recorded so many miraculous
events in his early life. The Welsh have never been content
with the unadorned data on David; they have enlarged his
figure with apocryphal episodes. The Israelites did the same
with the founder of their religion. Once the historical figure
of Moses as a revered leader and lawgiver had found a place
in Israel's traditions, it was in the narrator's interests to show

that his hero had been from the beginning a recipient of divine favor.

But if we conclude that the stories surrounding the birth of Moses are far from being factual accounts and were written from a didactic rather than a historical standpoint, what theological and educational purpose do they serve, apart from giving the hero credibility in the eyes of later generations? Two come to mind. The first centers around the activity of a group of women. The pharaoh's attempts to influence the course of history are foiled by five individuals who refuse to cooperate with him. All of them defy the oppressor and risk their lives to save the infant. Three of them, the midwives and the princess, act out of compassion and in accordance with the dictates of conscience. The mother proves to be resourceful and the sister quickwitted. Between them they form "a ring of tenderness" around the threatened child. Their actions determine the outcome of the episode. Liberation from bondage begins with them. They save the one whom God will choose to be the deliverer of his people. The possibility, based on these chapters, of reconstructing a biblical society that recognizes that women have a key role in God's plan for his world and records how they used their talents at crucial moments in the nation's history is welcomed by feminist theologians.

The second purpose is related to the Christian use of the Hebrew Scriptures. For the writers of the New Testament the infancy stories of Moses provide a framework for the messianic claims of Jesus. The birth of Moses prefigures that of the Savior. The Exodus story reminds the Christian of another cruel king, another slaughter of the innocents, another crucial family, another child in a cradle, and another trick that worked.

The Long March

The Israelites complained to Moses and Aaron in the wilderness
and said, "If only we had died at the Lord's hand in Egypt,
where we sat round the fleshpots and had plenty of bread to
eat! But you have brought us out into this wilderness to let this
whole assembly starve to death." . . . Moses told Aaron to say
to the whole community of the Israelites, "Come into the presence of the Lord, for he has heeded your complaints." While
Aaron was speaking to the community of the Israelites, they
looked towards the wilderness, and there was the glory of the
Lord appearing in the cloud. The Lord spoke to Moses and
said, "I have heard the complaints of the Israelites. Say to them,
'Between dusk and dark you will have flesh to eat and in the
morning bread in plenty. You shall know that I the Lord am
your God.' That evening a flock of quails flew in and settled
all over the camp, and in the morning a fall of dew lay all
around it. When the dew was gone, there in the wilderness,
fine flakes appeared, fine as hoar-frost on the ground. When
the Israelites saw it, they said to one another, "What is that?",
because they did not know what it was. Moses said to them,
"That is the bread which the Lord has given you to eat. This

is the commandment the Lord has given: 'Each of you is to gather as much as he can eat: let every man take an omer a head for every person in his tent.' The Israelites did this, and they gathered, some more, some less, but when they measured it by the omer, those who had gathered more had not too much, and those who had gathered less had not too little. Each had just as much as he could eat. Moses said, "No one may keep any of it until morning." Some, however, did not listen to Moses; they kept part of it till morning, and it became full of maggots and stank, and Moses was angry with them. Each morning every man gathered as much as he could eat, and when the sun grew hot, it melted away.

Exodus 16:2-3, 9-21

WHEN WE FIRST MEET THE ISRAELITES in the Bible, they are a people without a home. Throughout the Pentateuch, the first five books of the Hebrew Scriptures, they are depicted as a group of nomads always on the move, looking for a land promised them by God. Since most of this wandering period, which according to tradition lasted forty years, was spent in the wilderness, it is not surprising that the desert is the geographical setting of much of Exodus and the whole of Leviticus, Numbers, and Deuteronomy. It is only in the Book of Joshua that Israel finally reaches Canaan. The amount of space given to the wilderness episode in the biblical record demonstrates that it was regarded as one of the major traditions of ancient Israel. The account of the journey is found in two separate sections, one preceding the giving of the Law on Mount Sinai (Exod. 15–18) and one following it (Num. 10:11ff.). It is not clear why the author told part of the story before recording the making of the covenant on Sinai when, chronologically at least, the whole of it would take its place more naturally later on.

Despite its prominence within the Pentateuch, later biblical sources cannot agree about the significance that should be accorded to this particular period in the nation's history. Some agree with the authors of Exodus and Numbers and regard the forty wilderness years as a time of persistent and deeply ingrained rebelliousness, when Israel complained incessantly about God's harsh treatment of it. The Book of Psalms provides a good example:

How often they rebelled against him in the wilderness
and grieved him in the desert!
Again and again they tried God's patience
and provoked the Holy One of Israel. (Ps. 78:40-41)

The presence of this negative interpretation in the nation's sacred songbook suggests that it was both popular and familiar. But other sources speak fondly of the desert journey, regarding the forty years as a kind of honeymoon period for God and Israel. When Jeremiah exhorts the people of Jerusalem to turn away from idolatry, he reminds them of the commitment and faithfulness of their forefathers six hundred years previously:

These are the words of the Lord:
I remember the unfailing devotion of your youth,
the love of your bridal days,
when you followed me in the wilderness,
through a land unsown.
Israel then was holy to the Lord,
the first fruits of his harvest;
no one who devoured him went unpunished,
evil always overtook them. (Jer. 2:2-3)

For our present purpose we shall follow the interpretation

of the psalmist and regard the wilderness period as one of recalcitrance and disobedience characterized by the "murmuring" tradition — the term used in traditional translations for the motif of complaint and conflict that is so prominent throughout the episode. Although the Israelites do not go beyond verbal protest initially, their opposition to the liberation process gathers momentum, and they eventually threaten violence. Moses is faced with a counterrevolution. Within the Pentateuch the story appears in two forms: event and interpretation. On the one hand the bare facts are recorded in order to provoke wonder and sober reflection in the reader. On the other hand the experience is interpreted and used by the authors as a text for a sermon, as a means of instructing their contemporaries in theological truth. Of the two forms, the second is the more important. The true significance of the story is not to be sought in the factual details of what happened but in the transcendent meaning of the events. The story was told not simply to recall the past, for much of what took place was not worth recalling. It was included in Scripture as a lesson to those who came later. The account represents the episode as it was pondered and reflected upon by succeeding generations.

The details of the wanderings will not concern us here. We shall concentrate rather on the transcendent meaning that the authors of the Pentateuch — writing as they did with the benefit of hindsight — saw in the murmuring tradition and on the value of their insight for the Christian reader. Although it incites the people to rebel, the desert is of theological significance because it is the stage on which God's presence and power are revealed.

Rebellion

Because the wilderness generation is remembered for its disobedience, it is always compared unfavorably with the patri-
archs. The liberated slaves were the complete antithesis of
Abraham, Isaac, and Jacob, who were models of faith. They
had been in the desert only three days when they began to
complain about the quality of the water they were expected to
drink (Exod. 15:22-25). They soon found fault with Moses and
Aaron for bringing them out of Egypt and wished that they
had never left. They began to see the whole undertaking not
as a liberation project, but as a death project. The two brothers,
both of them in their eighties, had led six hundred thousand
fighting men, together with their wives and children, safely
through the Red Sea, and they were accused of betrayal. On
the journey from Sinai to Edom the people were so disillusioned and frightened that they began to talk about choosing
another leader to take them back to Egypt (Num. 14:4). But
the greatest act of rebellion was at Massah and Meribah, when
they challenged the Lord to prove once and for all that he was
with them. In their despondency they were driven to ask, "Is
the Lord in our midst or not?" (Exod. 17:7). According to
Numbers 14:22 this testing of God happened ten times.

What accounts for such ungracious behavior? Why were
the Israelites so anxious to return to the land of captivity and
forfeit the opportunity of entering the land of promise? One
reason is that the unexpected had come upon them. The long
period of wandering came as a very great shock to Israel. The
promise of deliverance, followed by a near idyllic existence in
a land flowing with milk and honey, a promise God had made
to Moses before he returned to Egypt (Exod. 3:7-8), contained
no mention of a gruelling march through harsh and hostile
country. Nothing had been said about wandering in circles for

forty years, living on iron rations. Consequently the Israelites had taken the Exodus to be the first fruits of freedom in a secure and fertile land. But things turned out differently. Reality fell short of promise — as it so often does. Somehow there had been a grave miscalculation, which had led to suffering and deprivation. Life in the wilderness began to take on a permanent aspect. The unexpected had come upon the disillusioned nomads, and they rebelled against it.

We witness exactly the same reaction hundreds of years later when the nation was exiled to Babylon. The capture of Jerusalem by the Babylonian king Nebuchadnezzar in 586 BC and the subsequent destruction of the temple took the inhabitants completely by surprise. Despite prophetic warnings, the people of Judah were totally unprepared for such a catastrophe simply because it did not coincide with popular belief. As God's chosen people, they believed themselves to be invulnerable. However lamentable the moral state of the nation, they were firmly persuaded that they would never be harmed. A poet recalls the experience:

> By the rivers of Babylon we sat down and wept
> when we remembered Zion.
> There on the willow trees we hung up our harps,
> for there those who carried us off
> demanded music and singing,
> and our captors called on us to be merry:
> "Sing us one of the songs of Zion."
> How could we sing the Lord's song in a foreign land?
>
> (Ps. 137:1-4)

The despondent exiles, convinced that God had deserted them, abandoned their instruments of worship. In a state of shock at the unexpected turn of events, faith eroded and trust turned to resentment. Survival as a community of loyal believers in an inhospitable environment was problematic.

The Book of Job provides another excellent example of rebellion, this time by an individual, in response to the unexpected. Though Job is "a man of blameless and upright life . . . who feared God and set his face against wrongdoing" (1:1), he suffers great torment. In his distress he curses the day of his birth and takes God to task for being silent and aloof. He berates him for his injustice and cruelty. He is certain that despite his integrity God will abandon him to his fate:

> I know that thou wilt hand me over to death,
> to the place appointed for all mortal men.
> Yet no beggar held out his hand
> but was relieved by me in his distress.
> Did I not weep for the man whose life was hard?
> Did not my heart grieve for the poor?
> Evil has come though I expected good;
> I looked for light but there came darkness. (Job 30:23-26)

Because he had been brought up to believe that bad things do not happen to good people, that the righteous are rewarded for their fidelity, Job's suffering was unexpected and therefore that much more poignant.

The unexpected, when it has an adverse effect, is never easy to cope with. Should it come upon us in the form of a bereavement, ill health, the loss of a job, failure at work, or rejection by colleagues, our natural reaction is to protest: "Why me? If only I had been warned." A wilderness experience can lead to disillusionment and often to rebellion.

But there is another, equally prominent, reason for the bad behavior of the wilderness generation: the people rebel because their needs are unfulfilled. As soon as they leave the

42

shores of the Red Sea the Israelites find themselves in a dangerous and hostile environment. Like all desert dwellers they live
in constant fear of death. Unlike arable land, the wilderness
has no "life support system"; it cannot provide life's basic necessities. "A land unsown," as Jeremiah calls the desert, offers
no sustenance for those who travel through it, because it is
lifeless. The wilderness is beyond cultivation; it is a land
without promise of security, it offers nothing but risks, the
greatest of which is hunger. "You have brought us out into this
wilderness to let this whole assembly starve to death" is the
opening accusation against the aged leaders. For Israel hunger
was the primary need, the one through which all others were
expressed. It was the trigger that sparked the rebellion.

Physical hunger has been described as a "total experience."
Unless it is quickly satisfied, it takes over the whole person.
An infant will become disorientated and irritable if he is hungry;
feed him and he will recover his equilibrium — he might even
sleep! A hungry man will spend every waking hour trying to
satisfy his need for food. The kind of third-world hunger reported on our television screens, with pictures of endless lines
of malnourished people queuing for a bowl of rice, is something
that the West knows nothing about. We may have skipped a
meal or two, but we have never experienced real hunger. But
when we realize through the media what hunger can do to
whole communities, it is hardly surprising that lack of food is
a prime cause of revolution in many developing countries. A
starving man or woman will go to any lengths to provide food
for self and family, for hunger is a total experience.

Physical hunger is of course only one form of hunger. More
subtle, though equally pervasive, is emotional or spiritual
hunger, a hunger for love, sympathy, acceptance, and recognition. Of whatever kind it is, hunger is an expression of need, and
need is something from which none of us is exempt. No one is

absolutely self-contained. A human being is in fact a cluster of needs, ranging from the basic need for food, which is common to everyone, to complex psychological needs, which vary from person to person. In a perceptive chapter on the many meanings of hunger, Monica Hellwig writes thus of the physical variety:

> Hunger is the most basic experience of dependence, of contingency, of the need for others. To be hungry is to experience oneself as insufficient, as having needs, as being unable to guarantee one's own existence. To be hungry is to know in a dark, inchoate kind of way that we do not create ourselves, but are creatures, receiving our existence as gift. Never really to be hungry is to be in danger of forgetting that our very existence is a gift — in danger of forgetting reverence and gratitude to the source of our being, the transcendent creator. It is not by accident that food, side by side with birth and death, has always been a central occasion for human communities to pray.[1]

Needs are a vital part of our makeup because they are our system of communication with the outside world, a purpose that they serve in at least two ways. First, by evoking the desire for satisfaction, they pinpoint the absence of something that is indispensable for our well-being. Many things remain outside our orbit until we actually need them. It is only when we are sick that we discover the need for medicine, it is only when we are lonely that we recognize our need for company. Shakespeare reminds us that "the jewel that we find we stoop and take 't because we see it; but what we do not see we tread upon, and never think of it."[2] We are unaware of many things

---

1. Monica Hellwig, *The Eucharist and the Hunger of the World* (New York: Paulist Press, 1976), p. 13.
2. Shakespeare, *Measure for Measure*, II:1.

until we need them. Second, our needs determine our actions. We can shut ourselves off from our environment if we wish, but sooner or later our needs will force us to come into contact with other people. Whether it is to ask for help or to rebel will depend on the circumstances.

Faced with what seems literally to be a godforsaken place that can never support them, the Israelites long to return to Egypt. Though ironic, such a longing does make sense. Slavery had many drawbacks, but it provided security. Slaves had cruel masters, but they were adequately fed, clothed, and housed. Life in the service of the pharaoh had not been easy, but it was familiar and reliable. There is a kind of freedom in bondage. Even the manna that God provided for their daily sustenance did not compare with the menu they had grown accustomed to in Egypt. The bread of liberation only generated a longing for the meat of slavery. "Will no one give us meat? Think of it! In Egypt we had fish for the asking, cucumbers and water-melons, leeks and onions and garlic. Now our throats are parched; there is nothing wherever we look except this manna" (Num. 11:5-6). The fleshpots of Egypt were infinitely preferable to the empty desert larder. In the original Hebrew the word translated "fleshpots" in Exodus 16:3 appears in the singular as "pot of flesh" and as such may refer to the actual eating of meat, though it should be borne in mind that in most cultures meat has been the food of the wealthy. In the plural, however, the word has a different connotation. It refers not to a number of pots containing meat, but to high living and sensual pleasures. Whatever the precise meaning in this context, the narrator wishes to indicate that the former slaves remembered life in Egypt as one of luxury.

This description of Egyptian slavery is, surely, a selective and idealized memory. But the fantasy is understandable, for the frightened travelers had a slave mentality. Dispirited and

45

degraded by years of oppression, they had lost the will to rebel. While they were in bondage to the pharaoh, they could not imagine any other possibility or envisage a situation that would bring freedom. Intimidation by their oppressors had made them fearful of taking the opportunity to be free; they were unwilling to face the risks of liberation, as Exodus 6:9 demonstrates only too clearly. When Moses repeated God's promise of deliverance to the captives, "they would not listen to him because their spirit had been broken by their cruel slavery." The determination to fight for their rights had been bred out of them, with the result that they were incapable of even hoping for liberation.[3] So when the opportunity came to leave Egypt, they failed to grasp it because they were psychologically conditioned to depend on their taskmasters. Submission had deprived them of initiative and self-respect. They were incapable of expressing anger at their situation. They preferred oppression and plenty to austerity and freedom. Little wonder that they regretted leaving Egypt and could not face the rigors of the desert.

The constant complaining, however, suggests more than nostalgia. It contains a direct criticism of the leadership. The people refuse to respect the judgment of Moses and Aaron and blame them for the inefficient way in which they have handled the whole affair. They lack enthusiasm for the enterprise because they have no confidence in their leaders' ability to avoid a catastrophe. This lack of faith in the emissary, the one sent by God to bring about the liberation and lead Israel to Canaan, is noted by Severino Croatto in his discussion of the important role human mediation plays in the faith process. Already, in Exodus 6:9, the Israelites had blocked God's plan by refusing

3. For an elaboration of this point see P. Freire, *Pedagogy of the Oppressed* (New York: Herder and Herder, 1970).

to recognize Moses' role or listen to his message. They did not realize that God reveals himself through a person as well as through events. "Moses is a key figure not only because he was the leader who successfully organized and led the departure from Egypt (as mediator) but also because he expresses an essential dimension of faith. It was easier for the Hebrews to believe in Yahweh [God] directly rather than in Moses, a human being like themselves. But this same God expressed himself through Moses."[4]

Belief in the emissary is fundamental to the biblical tradition. It undergirds the whole of the prophetic literature, for the prophet is the interpreter of God. It is equally significant in the New Testament. In John 5:43 Jesus complains that though the Scriptures testify to his coming, his contemporaries refuse to accept him: "I have come accredited by my Father, and you have no welcome for me." In Acts 7:2-53 Stephen defends himself before the Jewish court in Jerusalem by reminding his listeners that the Israelites had refused to believe in Moses even though he had been chosen by God to lead them to Canaan. He then condemns the Jews of his own day for rejecting Jesus and thereby doing just what their forefathers had done: "Like fathers, like sons. Was there ever a prophet whom your fathers did not persecute? They killed those who foretold the coming of the Righteous One; and now you have betrayed him and murdered him" (v. 52). Faith is expressed in the Bible in several ways. It appears, for instance, as the recognition of God's hand in certain historical events such as the Exodus and as commitment to the demands of the covenant made between God and his people on Sinai. But an important dimension is the recognition of and belief in God's emissary. By rejecting the emissary

4. J. Severino Croatto, *Exodus: A Hermeneutics of Freedom* (New York: Orbis Books, 1981), pp. 27f.

and refusing to accept his leadership, the wilderness generation was rejecting God.

Revelation

The experience of the unexpected, coupled with the realization that their needs were not going to be met, led Israel to rebel. The outward reason was physical hunger, but the true reason was spiritual hunger. Food crisis led to a faith crisis, for material and spiritual well-being are closely linked. The real issue revolved around the presence of God. "Is the Lord among us or not?" (Exod. 17:7) was the ultimate question. Was God with his people in the desert or was he still lingering in Egypt? This is the vital question that the biblical author seeks to answer. He insists that, despite all appearances, God is watching over his own. So the second major component in the wilderness story is the divine response to the nation's protest. Ostensibly this response takes the form of providing food, but essentially it is an answer to the question of presence. In response to the people's lack of faith God says to Moses, "I have heard the complaints of the Israelites. Say to them, 'Between dusk and dark you will have flesh to eat and in the morning bread in plenty. You shall know that I the Lord am your God'" (Exod. 16:11-12). The provision of food becomes a demonstration of presence in three ways.[5]

First, it brings satisfaction. The author of Deuteronomy, in reviewing the nation's history, uses the story of the manna to show that for the whole of the wilderness period Israel lacked nothing. "The clothes on your backs did not wear out nor did your feet swell these forty years" (Deut. 8:4). Not a single blister

5. See further W. Brueggemann, *The Land* (London: SPCK, 1978), ch. 3.

on the whole journey! God responds graciously to Israel's cry and provides for every need. There is nourishment even in the desert. Through having its needs met, Israel comes to believe that God is with it. The nation experiences in the wilderness what it thought only Egypt could provide, namely, satisfaction and security. By providing food, God asserts his presence as a sustainer. By bringing his people from death to life, he transforms the situation. A place of annihilation becomes a place of abundance.

Today, as ever, the world's poor must give priority to the search for food. They have no option, for hunger is a total need. Great social and religious reformers have always realized the magnitude of this need, which is why inner-city churches offer free meals. For a starving person food is synonymous with salvation. God is present whenever the hungry are filled, wherever needs, of whatever kind, are met. He is to be found not only in the unusual but also in the mundane.

Secondly, because God is present whenever needs are met, the food acts as a sacrament. The manna and quail are "an outward and visible sign of an inward and spiritual grace." God appears in the most unexpected place at the most unlikely hour. He is not to be found in the serenity of the sanctuary on some special day or at a hallowed hour, but in the wilderness at breakfast time and supper time. Initially Israel had raised the question not of God's presence but of food, and he had replied by giving them bread. But the food is a vehicle of his presence. Through it he enters the desolation of the desert to be with his people. "Bread-talk becomes God-talk." In the same way Christians experience the presence of God in the sacramental bread and wine of the Eucharist.

Finally, the provision of food teaches dependence. In the very place where the Israelites expect to die of hunger, they survive. In a land that lacks everything, they lack nothing because God has provided. They are forced to recognize their dependence on divine help because the bread that is provided is just enough to satisfy their daily requirements; there is never too much. Everyone receives a day's ration at a time; each man is given enough to meet his personal needs and those of his family, and no more. "Each of you is to gather as much as he can eat: let every man take an omer a head for every person in his tent." Inevitably some are greedy and collect more than they are entitled to. But when the amounts are measured, it is discovered that every person has received an omer apiece. Regardless of the energy expended in collecting it, the head of each family discovers that he can take home only the prescribed amount. There is equality at the checkout. Despite Moses' express instructions that none of the manna is to be kept until the following morning, some of the people try to hoard it. But it becomes stale and inedible; it has no shelf life. God's help is provided on a day-to-day basis. The manna is quite literally "daily bread." Israel is never allowed to live in total security even for one single day lest it forget its total dependence on God. Throughout the wilderness period the nation must be content with receiving a day's ration at a time. "The Israelites ate the manna for forty years until they came to a land where they could settle; they ate it until they came to the border of Canaan" (Exod. 16:35). Divine help does not miraculously change the wilderness into a paradise; neither the risk nor the dependence can be forgotten even for one moment. Each day has to be faced anew in faith. The manna is a sign that God is present and invites his people's trust.

The story of the long desert march is one of rebellion and revelation, of doubt and deliverance. It is a story of how God's chosen people lost and found their faith. If it is true that stories have their rightful place in religion and that faith builds on the experience of the centuries, this account of Israel's beginnings is not without relevance for us. All thinking Christians will at some point find themselves in the wilderness; they will have to endure the dark night of the soul. In such adverse circumstances perhaps the story we have just considered will help. Perhaps it will lead to the kind of faith expressed by the author of Psalm 23, who said with conviction, "The Lord is my shepherd; I shall want nothing." This too was the experience of the wilderness generation.

The Perils of an Interregnum

When the people saw that Moses was so long in coming down from the mountain, they confronted Aaron and said to him, "Come, make us gods to go ahead of us. As for this fellow Moses, who brought us up from Egypt, we do not know what has become of him." Aaron answered them, "Strip the gold rings from the ears of your wives and daughters, and bring them to me." So all the people stripped themselves of their gold earrings and brought them to Aaron. He took them out of their hands, cast the metal in a mould, and made it into the image of a bull-calf. "These," he said, "are your gods, Israel, that brought you up from Egypt." Then Aaron was afraid and built an altar in front of it and issued this proclamation, "Tomorrow there is to be a pilgrim-feast to the Lord." Next day the people rose early, offered whole-offerings, and brought shared-offerings. After this they sat down to eat and drink and then gave themselves up to revelry. But the Lord said to Moses, "Go down at once, for your people, the people you brought up from Egypt, have done a disgraceful thing; so quickly have they turned aside from the way I commanded them. They have made themselves an image of a bull-calf, they have prostrated themselves before *it, sacrificed to it and said, 'These are your gods, O Israel, that brought you up from Egypt.'" So the Lord said to Moses, "I have considered this people, and I see that they are a stubborn people. Now, let me alone to vent my anger upon them, so that I may put an end to them and make a great nation spring from you." But Moses set himself to placate the Lord his God: "O Lord," he said, "why shouldst thou vent thy anger upon thy people, whom thou didst bring out of Egypt with great power and a strong hand? Why let the Egyptians say, 'So he meant evil when he took them out, to kill them in the mountains and wipe them off the face of the earth'? Turn from thy anger, and think better of the evil thou dost intend against thy people. Remember Abraham, Isaac and Israel, thy servants, to whom thou didst swear by thy own self: 'I will make your posterity countless as the stars in the sky, and all this land, of which I have spoken, I will give to them, and they shall possess it for ever.'" So the Lord relented, and spared his people the evil with which he had threatened them.*

Exodus 32:1-14

*At Horeb they made a calf
and bowed down to an image;
they exchanged their Glory
for the image of a bull that feeds on grass.*

Psalm 106:19-20

THIS STORY, MORE THAN ANY OTHER in the Old Testament, has caused Jewish commentators acute difficulty. The fact that the honeymoon period in Israel's relationship with God was such a disaster proved to be a major predicament for later generations. It left them with a lot of explaining to do. Within months of becoming God's chosen people, the Israelites had apostatized; they had exchanged the Lord for an idol. Yet, despite such shameful behaviour, the rabbis felt duty-bound to excuse the action of their forefathers on account of the high regard in which they held those early pioneers. But however cogent their explanations, the sin of the golden calf remained unatoned, with disastrous consequences for Israel. In the opinion of the rabbis, the incident bequeathed a permanent legacy to the Jewish people; the repercussions would be felt for all time. From the Christian standpoint the story serves to accentuate the dark side of religion by demonstrating the harm it can do.

An Embarrassing Story

The fact that Israel so readily turned its back on God and worshipped an idol was a major stumbling block for the rabbis because it highlighted the faithlessness of the fathers during what many would consider to be the nation's golden age. According to ancient Jewish tradition, the calf was fashioned in imitation of the Egyptian bull-god, Apis. The Israelites were reverting to the god they used to worship before they were liberated, which suggests that they were ready to return to Egypt. Such blatant apostasy was hard to comprehend; it was even harder to understand why it was ever recorded. As it stands, the story constitutes a rupture of major proportions in the narrative of the Pentateuch, as the position of chapters 32–34 within the Book of Exodus indicates. The second half of the book, chapters 19–40, describes the revelation on Sinai, the giving of the Law, the sealing of the covenant and the making of the tabernacle — the portable shrine that symbolized God's presence among his people. But between the planning stage of the tabernacle (chapters 25–31), and the building of it (chapters 35–40), we find a record of the nation's apostasy. When all seemed to be progressing smoothly the people committed idolatry. The very ones who, in response to a reading of the covenant by Moses, said, "All that the Lord has spoken we will do, and we will be obedient" (Exod. 24:7), had already broken their promise. The rabbis found such infidelity embarrassing and perplexing.

But the faithlessness of the people was not nearly as problematic as the action of Aaron. By rabbinic times Aaron had long been recognized as a national and religious hero. He was the revered ancestor of the temple priesthood, the father of the Levites. His part in the story reflected badly not only on the priesthood but on Jewry as a whole. Two elements in the story proved difficult to explain and accept. The first was his abdication of responsibility as a leader in acquiescing far too readily to the people's demand. When the Israelites asked for an idol that would represent the God who was to lead them through the desert, Aaron cooperated without hesitation. He seemed to accept the status quo as permanent. He even built an altar in front of the calf on which the people could offer sacrifices. The Israelites were aided and abetted in their disobedience by God's own spokesman. The second was Aaron's careless use of language. His choice of verbs to describe his action in verse 24, "I threw it [the gold] in the fire and out came this bull-calf," implied that the idol simply appeared without human assistance. The phrase could therefore be taken to mean that the calf was a living entity, a concept that was calculated to give those who wanted to denigrate Judaism the opportunity to do so. Aaron should have expressed himself more carefully.

With the growth of anti-Judaism the story became even more disconcerting for the rabbis, in that both pagans and Christians used it to discredit the Jews and their religion. It became a useful source of anti-Jewish polemic. Because no one was allowed into the Holy of Holies, the inner sanctum of the Jerusalem temple, there was much speculation among non-Jews as to what was inside it. One theory, mentioned by pagan authors, was that it contained an ass's head made of gold that was discovered by the Greeks when they raided the Temple in 175 BC. In the pagan mind, the story of the ancient Israelites worshipping a golden calf helped to give credence to such a theory.

The anti-Judaism of the early Christians contained three main strands or charges, each of which has persisted down the centuries to modern times, namely deicide, diabolization, and displacement, all of which find support in the story of the golden calf. In Christian eyes, deicide, the killing of God, was the major crime of the Jews; it was the culmination of centuries of wickedness and disobedience. Though the New Testament writers do not mention it as such, Stephen comes close to doing so in his speech in Acts 7:2-53, which contains a fierce denunciation of the Jews for their wickedness. He lists a catalog of crimes that ends with the betrayal and murder of "the Righteous One," Jesus of Nazareth. In Stephen's mind, there is a clear progression from making of the calf to astral worship, from child sacrifice to the pagan god Moloch and the crucifixion of Jesus (7:40ff.). The sin of the golden calf therefore stood at the fountainhead of the crimes committed by the Jews throughout their history. In early Christian thought it was linked directly to deicide.

The episode also served to demonstrate that the Jews were in league with Satan. For St. Augustine, Moses' action in grinding the calf to powder, mixing it with water, and making the people drink it (Exod. 32:20) had the properties of a sacrament. Just as those who ate the consecrated bread are united with Christ, so the worshippers of the idol became one with the devil, represented by the calf. Thus the story became the cornerstone of the medieval identification of the Jew with Satan. Scripture itself testified to the diabolization of the Jews.

Finally, the creation of the calf proved that Israel had lost the claim to be God's covenant people, another crucial point in the Church's anti-Jewish polemic. The Old Israel had been displaced by the New Israel. The Christians regarded the episode as evidence that the covenant between God and Israel had been broken at the very dawn of the nation's history. The first set of commandments, which Moses had flung to the ground in anger at seeing the calf, had been shattered before the people ever received them. So the rejected status of the Jews can be traced to this story. The only covenant remaining in force was the covenant of Jesus. The Jews had become God's forsaken people. God hated them and would never forgive them.

The Bible makes no effort to excuse Israel's action or to mitigate its guilt. In fact, the crime is condemned unsparingly. But this very condemnation was yet another problem for the rabbis. On the one hand they could not deny the negative biblical record, on the other they were determined to defend their nation, and therefore protect it from violent Christian polemic. They did so in three ways. First they attempted to suppress the story, as witnessed by the attitude of Flavius Josephus. Though strictly speaking Josephus does not belong to the rabbinic period, his testimony is not insignificant. A Jewish historian of the final decades of the first century AD who wrote an extensive history of his people, he did not have to worry about Christian anti-Judaism, for in his day it was only in its infancy, but he was concerned with pagan prejudice. He would have been aware of the connection between the story of the golden calf and the pagan charge of Jewish idolatry. So in his history of the Jews, detailed though it is, he omits the story altogether. He was determined not to give pagans any opportunity to ridicule Jews. Clearly, for Josephus the sin of the golden calf was a sensitive issue.

The primary goal of the early and medieval rabbinic commentators was the vindication of Aaron. The rabbis noted that he was chosen by God to be High Priest *after* he had made the calf; his offense, therefore, could not have been major. The bestowal of priestly privileges upon him showed that God had not rejected him. As a result, his defense became a theological necessity, and several strenuous attempts were made to explain his action, and even exonerate him by putting the blame on others. For example, the claim is made that the people were threatening to kill him and that Aaron acquiesced to their demand to prevent them from committing a further and more serious crime. The rabbis point to his deliberate procrastination in asking for the people's jewelery, supposing that they would be unwilling to make such a major sacrifice. He then refused help to build the altar in front of the calf, thus ensuring that he would take an inordinately long time to complete it. He delayed as long as he could in the hope that Moses would return. Far from being condemned, Aaron was to be commended for his action. Furthermore, he built the calf in order to identify idolaters among the people; it was a deliberate trap laid by a shrewd man. It is also suggested that Aaron played no real part in the proceedings. The reference in verse 24 to a calf jumping out of the fire could be taken to imply that he did not actually make the idol himself; he only melted the gold.

The rabbis extended Aaron's innocence to Israel as a whole. In order to counter Christian arguments and raise Jewish morale, explanations had to be given for the people's action. One was that they were misled by Satan into believing that Moses was dead. Another was that two Egyptian magicians from among the "mixed company of strangers who had joined the Israelites" (Num. 11:4) when they left Egypt were responsible for building the calf and leading the people astray; the nation as such had nothing to do with it. This is deduced from the words "these are your gods, O Israel, that brought you up from Egypt," which must have been spoken by foreigners; if they had been Aaron's words they would have read "these are our gods." But even if they were guilty, the Israelites could never be blamed for breaking the Law by building the calf, because the Law had not yet been given — the ten commandments were withdrawn *before* Israel had received them. The breaking of the tables was a deliberate ploy on the part of Moses to keep the people in a state of innocence.

But the rabbis go further. In their attempt to exonerate both the nation and its leader, they even blame God for the catasrophe, claiming that if it was anyone's fault it was his for allowing Israel the opportunity to sin. After all, he had enslaved the people in Egypt, a land of idols, and had provided them with silver and gold on their release.

> Meanwhile the Israelites had done as Moses had told them, asking the Egyptians for jewellery of silver and gold and for clothing. As the Lord had made the Egyptians well-disposed towards them, they let them have what they asked; in this way they plundered the Egyptians. (Exod. 12:35-36)

He should have foreseen the problem that would arise when he told them to despoil the Egyptians. Referring to the incident, one rabbinic response reads as follows:

> It can be compared to a wise man who opened a perfumery shop for his son in a street frequented by prostitutes. The street did its work, the business also did its share; and the boy's youth contributed its part, with the result that he fell into evil ways. When his father came and caught him with a prostitute, he

began to shout, "I'll kill you." But his friend who was there said: "You ruined this youth's character and yet you shout at him! You ignored all other professions and taught him only to be a perfumer, you foresook all other districts and opened a shop for him just in a street where prostitutes dwell!" This is what Moses said: "Lord of the Universe! You ignored the entire world and caused your children to be enslaved only in Egypt, where all worshipped [idols], from whom your children learned [to do corruptly]. It is for this reason that they have made a calf! . . . Bear in mind whence you have brought them forth." (*Midrash Rabbah:* Exodus 43:7)

It was all God's fault. Not that he directly caused the building of the calf, but surely he knew the law of cause and effect.

Despite their ingenious defense of the Exodus generation in the face of Christian propaganda, the rabbis did make some pointed admissions. They unanimously agreed that the creation of the golden calf was one of the worst calamities in Jewish history. The seriousness of the act can be measured by its consequences. Even great national disasters were laid at the feet of the golden calf. The abolition of the monarchy, the loss of the priesthood, the destruction of the temple, the permanent exile of the Jews from their land, are all believed to be a direct result of worshipping the idol. A verse from the Babylonian Talmud sums it up: "No punishment ever comes upon Israel in which there is not a part payment for the sin of the golden calf." Some modern Jewish theologians have traced even the Holocaust to this single act of idolatry purported to have taken place over three thousand years ago.

The Dark Side of Religion

Despite the magnitude of Israel's crime and its permanent legacy, there were, according to the rabbis, extenuating circumstances. But this need for an apology only serves to highlight the difficulty, in religious terms, occasioned by the story. This surely prompts one to ask, Why is it in Scripture? Far more complimentary stories, found now only in the Apocrypha, were omitted from the Hebrew Bible. Why was this one included? More to the point, why is it read in Christian churches during divine service? Well, perhaps because it says something about the nature of religion that we might do well to heed. By accentuating the negative it emphasizes the danger inherent in every religious persuasion. As Rabbi Lionel Blue has pointed out forcefully in one of his radio talks, "A lot of religion is not just worthless: it is positively harmful. Just because the word 'religion' or 'God' is used on the headed notepaper does not mean that He is in anything of what is written. It could be a fraud, which in any other business would be an offence under the Trade Descriptions Act."[1]

In the context of the harm caused by religion, the Jesuit teacher and writer Gerard Hughes refers to the false notions of sin and repentance propagated by the Roman Catholic Church. Bad teaching can leave the impression on the minds of children and adults that God has sown a minefield along the believer's path and entrusted the map to the clergy. The opportunities of stepping on a mine are innumerable. Deliberately missing Mass on Sunday, for instance, "can incur an eternal sentence in conditions which would make the Gulag Archipelago seem like a luxury hotel in comparison." Alongside this threat of hell and

1. Lionel Blue, *Bright Blue: Rabbi Lionel Blue's Thoughts for the Day* (London: BBC, 1985), p. 70.

damnation a complicated casuistry developed to enable the faithful to negotiate the minefield without losing a limb. Hughes concludes his observation thus:

> The damage done to a sensitive and imaginative person by this kind of teaching is tragic and a perversion of the Good News. Having listened to one particular person who had suffered inner torture through this kind of teaching, I was not at all surprised when, in answer to my question, "If you were completely free of all moral obligation, what would you most like to do?", she answered, "Burn down churches."[2]

From the other end of the denominational spectrum an Anglican theologian in the evangelical tradition, whose wife is a psychologist, claims that many Evangelicals develop a style of preaching and counseling that aims to destroy any human self-confidence and a sense of personal worth. In a chapter entitled "The Dark Side of Evangelicalism," he discusses, "the sense of guilt, paralysis and self-doubt" generated by such a style. It creates Christians who "feel unable to do anything for God, for others, or for themselves. The counselling rooms of secular psychologists are full of Christians who have been destroyed by this kind of evangelical preaching."[3] The eminent American psychiatrist M. Scott Peck tells how he used to joke that churches of all denominations provided him with his livelihood, but "the fact of the matter is that psychotherapists must spend enormous amounts of time and effort in the struggle to liberate their patients' minds from outmoded religious ideas and concepts that are clearly destructive."[4] In an-

2. Gerard Hughes, *God of Surprises* (London: DLT, 1985), p. 67.
3. A. McGrath, *Evangelicalism and the Future of Christianity* (London: Hodder, 1988), p. 148.
4. M. Scott Peck, *The Road Less Travelled* (London: Arrow, 1978), p. 222.

cient religious movements and in the major churches, to say nothing of the sects, of our own day, the harm religion can do manifests itself in many ways. Three come to mind, based on this story.

The first is the rejection of tradition. Under Aaron's leadership, Israel turned its back on tradition. It substituted a golden calf for Jehovah, as the psalmist sarcastically points out. Modern religious movements always claim to be offering something new and different. The basic message may be the same as it always has been, or at least possess some of the original elements, but the packaging and presentation are very different. There is of course a positive aspect to this rejection, for not everything in the tradition is worth keeping. But when the need to reject becomes obsessive, when it becomes an article of the creed, as it invariably does in latter-day sects, it is harmful. It is harmful because it wrenches a person out of the environment in which he or she has grown up. The first thing that happens to people who join a sect is that they are brainwashed into thinking that everything they have believed in the past is quite erroneous. They are persuaded that the Christian tradition, as it developed over two thousand years, has neither value nor importance. We hardly need reminding of the untold misery such an attitude has brought to countless families — on notepaper headed "religion."

In the *Screwtape Letters* C. S. Lewis has some penetrating comments on the rejection of tradition. The senior devil writes to his nephew and disciple:

My dear Wormwood, . . . The real trouble with the sect your patient is living in is that it is merely Christian. They all have individual interests of course, but the bond remains mere Christianity. What we want, if men become Christians at all, is to keep them in a state of mind I call "Christianity and." You know — Christianity and the New Psychology, Christianity and Faith

Healing, Christianity and Psychical Research, Christianity and Vegetarianism, Christianity and Spelling Reform. If they must be Christians let them at least be Christians with a difference. Substitute for the faith itself some fashion with a Christian colouring. Work on their horror of the Same Old Thing. The horror of the Same Old Thing is one of the most valuable passions we have produced in the human heart — an endless source of heresies in religion, folly in counsel, infidelity in marriage, and inconstancy in friendship.[5]

By inflaming the horror of the same old thing Screwtape and his assistants create a craving for novelty and change that causes havoc.

The second manifestation of the dark side of religion is the rejection of tolerance. In the story of the golden calf the absence of leadership is the starting point for action. One cannot but notice the derogatory and contemptuous tone of the Israelites when they refer to Moses in Exodus 32:1: "As for this fellow Moses . . . we do not know what has become of him." Later this disrespect turned into open rebellion and only just stopped short of murder. The people found it difficult to tolerate Moses simply because he did not agree with them. Religious institutions suffer from exactly the same weakness. They manipulate God, they make him partial, they insist that he has his favorites. They can be uncompromising in their beliefs because invariably they have a direct line to the throne of grace. To preserve their purity, the faithful are strictly forbidden any meaningful contact with those considered to be beyond the pale. Such fanatic intolerance does not help people to grow in sympathy and understanding.

5. C. S. Lewis, *The Screwtape Letters* (London: Collins Fontana, 1959), no. 25, p. 126.

But intolerance is not confined to sects. The eminent Scottish teacher and theologian William Barclay tells us in his autobiography, *Testament of Faith,* that for the last in a series of six radio meditations he spoke about his own personal faith and beliefs, alluding in passing to the recent death of his only daughter and her fiancée in a boating accident. The following week he received a letter from a member of one of the mainline Protestant churches in Northern Ireland expressing no surprise or sympathy for his bereavement, but claiming that the girl had been taken by God to save her from her father's heretical teachings.

There is a sense in which every revealed religion is potentially guilty of intolerance. Its special messages and its authoritarian manner have often caused the fragmentation of the tenuous unity of the human family. Faith and fanaticism can be, and often are, closely related. Vehemence of belief seems to be the inevitable opponent of tolerance. The firmer the belief, the more violent and irrational its propagation. For extremists, the toleration of dissent spells danger. It is only by being self-assured and anti-dialogue that their religion or denomination can withstand the assaults of modernity. A fragile faith gains strength from intolerance; witness the fact that faiths or Churches that show empathy for those with whom they disagree fail to prosper as much as those that do not. All the great religions preach love but are quite capable of practicing hatred; they talk about compassion to everyone, but actively encourage indifference, and worse, towards those of a different persuasion. There is undoubtedly some good religion in Ireland, Israel, Iran, and America, "but there is an awful lot of sick stuff which finds it easier to erect walls than to build bridges."[6] In Northern Ireland fundamentalist Protestant sects rant and rave about the

6. Blue, p. 70.

65

iniquities of the Roman Catholic Church, while in the Irish Republic that same church, because it claims the allegiance of 95 percent of the population, has in the past adopted a triumphalist and heavy-handed attitude in its treatment of religious minorities. Irish Protestants, Jews, and Muslims were not consciously discriminated against, but their sensibilities were certainly ignored.

In January 1995, some months after the ceasefire in Northern Ireland, the Anglican Archbishop of Armagh said this with reference to sectarianism, which, he claimed, was still strong in Ireland:

> Those who remain centred in the safety of the well-trodden path, proclaiming their revelation of God's purpose in terms of "what we have, we hold," are to be found in Ireland in both the Reformed and the Roman Catholic families. For them it is so often not just "if in doubt leave well alone" but rather "you change for we will not." Many aspects of the current peace process itself could fail if sectarianism is not faced for what it is. Sectarianism is still the greatest challenge to joint church action and the greatest problem for the Churches in Ireland, North and South. We have yet to understand how deep it lies in the consciousness of people, or to face up to ways of countering it.[7]

In Israel Orthodox Jews nurse an implacable hatred not only of Arab Christians, but of Reform Jews, all in the name of the God who said, "You shall love your neighbor as yourself." Five times a day the ayatollahs pray to Allah, the merciful, the compassionate, but they find it necessary to put every obstacle in the way of the small Iranian Church. The same intolerance on

7. As reported in the *Church Times,* 20 January 1995.

religious issues is found in many other countries. It may not always erupt into open violence, but it claims many casualties.

We reject tolerance at our peril, for such rejection can spawn a lethal bigotry, intense and unrelenting. Religious fanatics, who find it impossible to tolerate dissent, develop a siege mentality that prompts them to highlight the dangers inherent in questioning authority. Because identifying the Antichrist has become an obsession, they justify extremism by demonizing their opponents — as the Jews know to their cost. Organized religion is to blame for more misery and intolerance than mankind has suffered from any other source. With the revival of religious passions around the world, it is salutary to reflect on their destructiveness in the past. One must agree with Professor Hans Küng when he says that there will be no peace among nations without peace among religions and no peace among religions without dialogue between religions. Intolerance is no basis for dialogue.

The third manifestation is the rejection of truth. As soon as he had built the calf, Aaron pointed to it and said, "These are your gods, O Israel, who brought you up from Egypt." That, of course, was arrant nonsense, and he knew it. But the people believed him. They exchanged their glorious God for the image of a bull; they traded truth for falsehood. They believed what they wanted to believe, though they must have known it to be false. The psalmist may fulminate, but how easy it is to do just that. It is easy simply because the vast majority of people do not understand their faith intellectually. They do not think of it in intellectual terms; they do not question it. By this I am not suggesting that there should be an IQ test for confirmation, or that emotion has no place in religion. But there is room for discernment, for common sense. Many intelligent, sensible, and articulate people seem to have a blind spot in matters of faith and religion. In every other facet of life they apply the most rigorous standards, but in religion they seem to have no discernment. They may come from an ancient religious culture, but they seem to be incapable of detecting hocus-pocus when it stares them in the face. Because they clamor for religious certainty, they swallow the claptrap of cranky sects or embrace without question the biblical tyranny of an arid literalism. In many cases the light eventually dawns. They recognize "the spiritual thuggery of fundamentalism" and they break free to join a more enlightened group of Christians.

This unwillingness on the part of members to understand their faith intellectually puts a great burden on the leader. The leader of any faith or sect bears an awesome responsibility, simply because he or she has people who are hanging on his or her every word. The leader literally has the power of life and death over the followers — witness the mass suicide of a group of Americans some years ago in Latin America, and more recently the debacle at the headquarters of the ill-fated Branch Davidian cult in Texas. Sect members will take their own lives simply because they are told to. Admittedly the orders are given on paper headed "religion," but in actual fact those who obey them exchange "their Glory for the image of a bull that feeds on grass." If the leader is a dud, one of the first things to go will be the truth; it will be sacrificed in order to satisfy his or her own ego. Tragically, the vast majority of the followers fail to realize this. They know that any challenge to such autocracy will not be tolerated, but they neither appreciate how extensive the leader's power is nor realize how ready the leader is to use it to manipulate the weaker members of the group. Just as the Israelites were conned by Aaron, so today vast numbers of people are bamboozled by the religious jargon of unscrupulous men and women who are past masters at uncovering a person's vulnerability. Ritual and mystery are powerful tools in the hands of charlatans.

To conclude: In concentrating on a problematic story I have emphasized the negative side of religion, which, whether we like it or not, exists. Among the dangers inherent in any religious system is its rejection of tradition, tolerance, and truth. But I must not stop there. I am bound to note that the cloud has a silver lining. Even to the story of the golden calf there is a positive side. "So the Lord relented, and spared his people the evil with which he had threatened them." Before the story ends, we are provided with a testimony to God's forgiveness. Israel continued to exist because God picked up the pieces. There never was a period of unblemished saintliness; Israel was off the rails from the start. The only way to get onto them at all was by God's grace.

A Blueprint for Survival

*Today I offer you the choice of life and good, or death and evil.
If you obey the commandments of the Lord your God which I
give you this day, by loving the Lord your God, by conforming
to his ways and by keeping his commandments, statutes, and
laws, then you will live and increase, and the Lord your God
will bless you in the land which you are entering to occupy.
But if your heart turns away and you do not listen and you
are led on to bow down to other gods and worship them, I tell
you this day that you will perish; you will not live long in the
land which you will enter to occupy after crossing the Jordan.
I summon heaven and earth to witness against you this day: I
offer you the choice of life or death, blessing or curse. Choose
life and then you and your descendants will live; love the Lord
your God, obey him and hold fast to him: that is life for you
and length of days in the land which the Lord swore to give to
your forefathers, Abraham, Isaac and Jacob.*

Deuteronomy 30:15-20

IT WAS DAI BREAD, THE BAKER, that colorful character in Dylan Thomas's *Under Milk Wood* with two wives — one for the daytime and one for the night — who had above his bed, inscribed in three colors and gold leaf, the immortal words "God is love." But such framable and apposite texts are few and far between, especially so from the pages of the Old Testament. However, if you had asked the authors of the New Testament, and even Jesus himself, where they found most of their quotable quotes, they would have directed you to Deuteronomy. A nineteenth-century scholar counted eighty-three direct and indirect citations from this one book between the covers of the New Testament.

But of all the books in the Hebrew Bible, why Deuteronomy? Because for the ancient Israelite it was a blueprint for survival — the survival of both nation and faith. To say that about any book is to say enough to convince us of its relevance to our own age, an age for which survival, whether it be religious, cultural, national, or global, is a priority. It was written, many believe, towards the end of the seventh century, a time when the Israelites were standing at a critical juncture in their history. Under bad King Manasseh political and economic pressures had made the bribe and the compromise the constant companion of the merchant and the judge. God had been forgotten, even denied. The ancient faith had become distinctly decaffeinated. It was touch and go whether the religion of Jehovah would survive at all. And this disease, which had entered the very soul of the nation, was relentlessly pursuing its destructive course. The words of an earlier prophet, Hosea, are relevant to this period too: "You have sown the wind, you will reap the whirlwind."

Faced with this crisis, a group of men produced a document that offered their contemporaries another chance, and they called their finished product just that, *deuteros nomos,* the second law. They wrote under a pen name, that of Moses, for the book purports to be Moses' last sermon, containing instructions for the Israelites on how to live in Canaan when the wilderness wanderings are over. By claiming Mosaic authorship the compilers sought to add weight to their recommendations. But they did not fool anyone, for the ascription of books to famous people was by no means uncommon. A good example of such pseudonymity from a later period is *The Wisdom of Solomon,* found in the Apocrypha, which was written over eight hundred years after the death of the purported author.

The style and content of Deuteronomy indicate the book's provenance. In style it is sermonic or homiletic, that is to say, repetitive and exhortatory. Not surprisingly, it has been described as "preached law." In a comment on Deuteronomy 4 a noted biblical scholar writes:

> Who is it who speaks thus, so urgently, so broadly, so much from the heart, warning, promising, presupposing good intentions, repeating again and again what is well known, ethical and religious alike? It is not the prophet. His words are more tense, more definite, more decisive, fresher and more profound in form and content. Nor is it the popular speaker, for he speaks less religiously, more boldly, less clerically, more worldly, less sustainedly. It is the preacher who speaks thus. With the seventh century, the preacher begins to make his voice heard. The sermon, the greatest and best form of human instruction, comes into being.[1]

The authors of Deuteronomy were not lawyers but preachers, who used the law to teach the faith and provide moral guidance. The book is not a compendium of legal rulings produced for

---

1. L. Köhler, *Hebrew Man* (London: SCM, 1956), p. 158.

the benefit of legal experts, but a compilation of laws interspersed with instruction and exhortation designed for society at large. To call Deuteronomy a law book in the conventional sense is, therefore, to misrepresent its contents. It is more accurate to describe it as a collection of sermons based on ancient laws.

It must be appreciated that the authors wrote with the benefit of hindsight, all six hundred years of it. They knew that Israel had failed to keep the first law, given long ago on Sinai and enshrined in the Book of Exodus; the crisis through which they were living was, in their eyes, ample proof of that. So they presented their contemporaries with a blueprint for survival, what they might have called "the good news according to Moses." Three key concerns of the authors emerge from the book; in noting them we shall try to see their relevance for our own age.

Living

The promised land to which the Israelites are going features prominently throughout the book. The authors cannot conceive of life apart from the land. To put it in another way, they are very materialistic in their thinking, as indicated by their fulsome references to the fertility of Canaan and the high standard of living that such abundance guaranteed:

> For the Lord your God is bringing you to a rich land, a land of streams, of springs and underground waters gushing out in hill and valley, a land of wheat and barley, of vines, fig-trees, and pomegranates, a land of olives, oil and honey. It is a land where you will never live in poverty nor want for anything, a land whose stones are iron-ore and from whose hills you will

dig copper. You will have plenty to eat and will bless the Lord your God for the rich land that he has given you. (Deut. 8:7-10)

In thus praising the advantages of a settled existence and the material prosperity of an agricultural society, the book provides an important contrast to another way of regarding human life, namely that of life as a pilgrimage. The nomadic image pictures man as someone on the move towards a goal, someone who lives in the hope of a good time to come. The great exemplar is Abraham, who as the old evangelical hymn says, "nightly pitched his moving tent a day's march nearer home." The author of the letter to the Hebrews adopted this image and regarded the people of God on earth as pilgrims, people who in this world "have no permanent home," but "are seekers after the city which is to come" (13:14). As Christians we are properly warned against any kind of overattachment to material things and offered a life that is eternal and transcendent. If we forget this, the author of the First Letter to Timothy is at hand to remind us that "we brought nothing into the world" and that "we cannot take anything with us when we leave" (6:7). The pilgrim concept of Christian discipleship, which understands the temporal world as having value only as a preparatory stage for a life of celestial bliss, is frequently emphasized in the New Testament.

While this dimension must, of course, be recognized, the pilgrim image, like all images, has its dangers if taken in isolation. It has led some Christians to put too much stress on personal salvation, to look to the future at the expense of the present, and to speak of heaven far more than of earth. It has encouraged them to replace the Jewish hope of transforming this world with a promise of eternal life. Two examples of this otherworldly outlook will suffice. The first is from Latin America. For centuries the Roman Catholic Church in South America persuaded the poor to accept their lot patiently. It preached with assurance that all would be well in the long run, for earthly misery would be exchanged for heavenly joy. It interpreted the words of Jesus, "Blessed are the poor, for theirs is the kingdom of God," as meaning that poverty should be accepted as a way of life because injustice would be compensated for in the hereafter. The poor were reminded that they were pilgrims and therefore advised not to rock the boat by challenging the political structures that marginalized them, because living on the breadline had a positive theological value. The rich loved it.

In 1968 this way of thinking was challenged from within the Church itself. At a Bishops' Conference in Medellín, Colombia, a group of prominent theologians openly criticized the hierarchy's close links with the ruling elite and their lack of concern for the material welfare of the underprivileged. They called for liberation from all forms of oppression, whether it be political, economic, sexual, racial, or religious. They rejected a spirituality that was removed from the real world and that ignored the actual living conditions of the vast majority of the population. In fact they regarded such an outlook as positively harmful. In the words of one critic, "The hope of the Kingdom, far from awakening an ethos to transform the world in the direction of that which was expected, worked as a deterrent for historical action."[2] These theologians rejected a purely spiritual concept of God's Kingdom because they saw it as a means of avoiding Christian action. They saw history as the arena of God's saving acts and the demand for human rights as part of the transforming power of the gospel. They taught that God was concerned with life as we know it on earth and that when he brought his people out of Egypt he was liberating them not

2. J. Miguez Bonino, *Doing Theology in a Revolutionary Situation* (Philadelphia: Fortress, 1975), p. 133.

75

simply from sin and guilt, but from political oppression. They insisted that this God demanded justice, not the performance of ritual acts or subscription to the correct religious beliefs. In order to eliminate injustice they stressed that the Church must play its part in overthrowing the prevailing political and economic system. This was the genesis of what has become known as "liberation theology." Although this challenge is often referred to as a "movement," strictly speaking it is a specific way of doing theology.

But despite the profound impact liberationists have had on theological reflection worldwide, they have been taken to task by Evangelicals and Roman Catholics alike. The present pope disagrees radically with them. They are criticized for being dismissive of biblical scholarship, for mixing religion with politics, for being preoccupied with Marxism, and for propagating a theology that is human-centered rather than God-centered.

The second example concerns the Church of England. The appalling conditions under which many people in Britain worked during the nineteenth century are well known. When a few lone voices, namely the Christian Socialists and the Tractarians (the Anglican High Church party that was determined to take God to the slums), protested and called for a better deal, the reaction of the ecclesiastical authorities was very lukewarm. There may have been several reasons for such an attitude on the part of the authorities, but one of them was the fact that the Church had a theology that taught that life was a pilgrimage. Such thinking is reflected in the hymns written during the period. Their contents are worth noting, for hymnbooks are an excellent source of theology without tears. The famous hymn

Guide me O thou Great Redeemer
Pilgrim through this barren land,

was written in Welsh in 1750 by one of our greatest hymn writers and soon translated into English, so that others could join us in preaching that the best was yet to come.

> Through the night of doubt and sorrow
> onward goes the pilgrim band,
> Singing songs of expectation,
> marching to the promised land,

is another familiar hymn. Translated from the Danish, it was sung with great gusto in Queen Victoria's Britain while ten-year-old boys went down the mines and men and women sweated for a pittance in "those dark satanic mills." Faced with such obvious injustice, the established Church merely talked about a promised land where all would be well. And though the fact was never emphasized, everyone knew that the only way to get there was via the cemetery. But the British are not the only ones to blame. The white American plantation owner also taught the slaves to sing:

> This world is not my home,
> I'm just a-passin thru.

While keeping alive the dream of heaven, we are open to the criticism of aiding and abetting those who promote the conditions of hell. Our pilgrimage theology may be true to one aspect of New Testament teaching, but it is at risk of becoming distinctly lopsided because it fails to influence the present.

Returning to Deuteronomy, we find a totally different emphasis. The book concentrates throughout on the land, on the here and now. There is a concern about the quality of human life, which is seen in terms not of the hereafter, but of every person's inalienable right to enjoy God's gifts. We hear a positive affirmation of our continuing desire for a home, a place where we can live to our fullest potential. The enjoyment of home, family, work, and the fruits of one's labors is bound up with human existence; it is at least one of the legitimate goals of life. Material things, "the good land," are to be sought and cherished. Deuteronomy is concerned not with how things will turn out in the long run, but with how they actually are in the short run. A this-worldly concept of the Kingdom of God is deeply rooted in the Old Testament.

Such an emphasis is surely not alien to Christianity, for the Christian faith has been described, quite correctly, as the most materialistic of all religions. It is regarded thus because of the incarnation, because God actually became a human being. By sharing our nature, by "taking manhood into God," as Saint Athanasius says, God showed that human life matters. God's action in the Bible is located in the physical details of human life — slavery in Egypt, exile in Babylon, birth, pain, joy, the breaking of bread, and the drinking of wine. This is true Christian materialism, and as such, an essential part of the gospel. Flesh becomes the vehicle of salvation; matter becomes the means of revelation. The history of the Church, however, is marked by continuous attempts to reject Christian materialism in favor of an otherworldly spirituality — pilgrimage theology — in which matter becomes second rate. Christian leaders have attacked materialism as being reprehensible and have concentrated solely on the spiritual. But when William Booth went into the teeming slums of the British industrial cities at the end of the last century, he said that he took with him three things: soup, soap, and salvation, and added, "in that order." Deuteronomy would have said Amen to that.

Sharing

The vision of Deuteronomy demanded action. The book was not written by theologians looking out through the windows of an ivory tower. The authors were vitally in touch with the world of their day, and what is more, they knew what was in the heart of their fellow human beings. They knew how easily land and natural resources could be misused. While the privileged few hoarded and squandered material things, the poor were denied the basic necessities of life. If humans were to succeed in living life to the full, if they were to reap the maximum benefit from material wealth inherited and created, they must be persuaded to be generous and open, they must realize that life involves giving and sharing. So the authors issued a set of guidelines and stamped them with the divine imprimatur. These were not laws as we understand that term, but the bricks and mortar of a way of life. As we have already noted, they were presented not as a binding burden, but as a God-given source of guidance to enable the nation to manage and enjoy its land. They were seen as an expression of the divine grace, not as its counterpart. That is the true meaning of *Torah,* the Hebrew word that we translate as "Law."

The most prominent characteristics of the way of life set out here are compassion and generosity. The compassion inherent in Israelite law is to be found, for example, in the attitude towards animals. Though human beings have been entrusted by God with dominion over the created order (Gen. 1:28), this does not give them the right to exploit animals or be cruel to them. Jewish tradition states explicitly that humans are not to inflict pain on animals. Even on the Sabbath, when all but essential work is proscribed, the Law stipulates that assistance should be given to any animal in distress. "When you see your fellow-countryman's ass or ox lying on the road, do not ignore it; you must help him to lift it to its feet again" (Deut. 22:4). The duty of care is paramount.

Another aspect of this humaneness is a generosity that engenders in the human heart a respect for the natural order. "If you chance to come upon a bird's nest, in any tree or on the ground, with young ones or eggs and the mother sitting upon the young or upon the eggs, you shall not take the mother with the young; you shall let the mother go, but the young you may take to yourself; that it may go well with you, and that you may live long" (Deut. 22:6f.). Preserve the species and spare the next generation an environmental headache. Chapter 15:1 refers to the year of release: "At the end of every seventh year you shall make remission of debts." Originally the reference to "release" or "remission" was associated with an injunction not to cultivate the land for a year, a point that is made explicitly in Exodus and receives further elaboration in Leviticus 25:1-7. "For six years you may sow your land and gather its produce; but in the seventh year you shall let it lie fallow and leave it alone. It shall provide food for the poor of your people" (Exod. 23:10). Perhaps it is not too fanciful to regard this law also as a recommendation not to overwork the soil in an effort to become rich overnight. A field needs the occasional day off as much as humans do, so leave it fallow every seventh year. Resist the temptation to plough it to death and thereby avoid the problem of a dust bowl. For a generation that is becoming increasingly aware of the ecological mess it is in, no advice could be more timely.

There is also, of course, a generosity towards other people. Those who are comfortably off must ensure that the economically weak and the socially underprivileged receive a share of the good things of life. "When you gather the grapes from your vineyard, do not glean afterwards; what is left shall be for the alien, the orphan and the widow" (24:21). The three

80

groups of people mentioned here were those who, through no fault of their own, had no land, and were therefore dependent on others for their welfare. Israelite law took special measures to protect them and to ease their burden by commanding generosity. The relevance of this kind of legislation to our own age is too obvious to require elaboration. A very large percentage of the world's population still lives, quite literally, off the land. If the land fails for just one season, as it frequently does in some parts of the world, there is no food. Western consumer society, accustomed as it is to the availability of every commodity, finds this difficult to comprehend; Deuteronomy does not.

The exhortations of Deuteronomy point to a generosity that is the very antithesis of exploitation and avarice. They set limits to selfish excess by urging the reader not to be so anxious to turn everything back into greater profits. There is a fight in this book against "all that kills abundant living." I think it is Nicholas Berdayev who says that while the problem of my own bread is a material question, the problem of my neighbor's bread is a spiritual one. Every advantage each one of us has implies a responsibility, a moral responsibility, to share. We cannot make a success of our own lives unless we strive in every way to make a success of the lives of others. In the words of a modern hymn:

> For the healing of the nations,
> Lord, we pray with one accord;
> For a just and equal sharing
> Of the things that earth affords,
> To a life of love in action,
> Help us rise and pledge our word.

The authors of Deuteronomy would have said Amen to that.

Thanksgiving

With its obvious emphasis on every person's humanitarian duty to share the blessings of life, Deuteronomy's message is very materialistic. But it is a holy materialism, for the benefits are seen as the gifts of God; he is recognized as the giver behind the gift. In addition to being one of sharing, therefore, life had to be one of thanksgiving. The authors made a determined effort to bring back the beyond. They sought to give life that all-important spiritual dimension that it was rapidly losing. For they knew that however good life was materially speaking, that was not the whole story. "Man," they said, "cannot live on bread alone but lives by every word that comes from the mouth of the Lord" (8:3). Bread, yes, as much of it as possible, but let no one make the mistake of supposing that that is all there is to life.

Deuteronomy's emphasis on life's spiritual dimension manifests itself primarily in the call to remember:

> Take care not to forget the Lord your God and do not fail to keep his commandments, laws, and statutes which I give you this day. When you have plenty to eat and live in fine houses of your own building, when your herds and flocks increase, and your silver and gold and all your possessions increase too, do not become proud and forget the Lord your God who brought you out of Egypt, out of the land of slavery. . . . Nor must you say to yourselves, "My own strength and energy have gained me this wealth," but remember the Lord your God; it is he that gives you strength to become prosperous. (8:11-18)

This warning against forgetting the great acts of God on Israel's behalf, especially the Exodus, is given so forcefully and so frequently simply because the nation's failure to remember is at the root of all its problems. Prophets such as Amos and

Micah attribute the moral decline of the eighth century to precisely this issue. Disobedience to the demands of the Law stemmed from ingratitude, which in turn stemmed from the failure to recognize and remember God's gracious actions in the past.

Memory is vital to the Judeo-Christian tradition. According to Abraham Heschel, for the Jew to have faith is to remember. He writes:

> Memory is a source of faith. To have faith is to remember. Jewish faith is a recollection of that which happened to Israel in the past. The events in which the spirit of God became a reality stand before our eyes in colours that never fade. Much of what the Bible demands can be comprised in one word: *Remember*. . . . Jews have not preserved the ancient monuments, they have retained the ancient moments. The light kindled in their history was never extinguished. With sustaining vitality the past survives in their thoughts, hearts, rituals. Recollection is a holy act: we sanctify the present by remembering the past.[3]

The New Testament scholar Nils Dahl makes the same point when he discusses the nature of early Christianity: "The first obligation of the apostle, vis-à-vis the community — beyond founding it — is to make the faithful remember what they have received and already know — or should know."[4] Memory plays such a significant part in every historical religion because of what it effects. By appealing to their readers to remember the past, the authors of Deuteronomy sought to guide them into a better future. The memory of God's goodness to the fathers

3. A. J. Heschel, *Man Is Not Alone* (New York: Farrar, 1951), p. 161.
4. Quoted by Henri Nouwen, *The Living Reminder* (New York: Seabury, 1977), p. 13.

would, if preserved, ensure that Israel honored its side of the covenant relationship.

But the call to remember is not the only evidence of the spirituality of Deuteronomy. Prominence is also given to motivation and intention. While right action is of supreme importance, the mind and the heart are of equal significance. While many, if not most, commandments are concerned with orthopraxy (acting in the correct way) there are those that are concerned with inner experiences — with thoughts, attitudes, feelings, and dispositions. The following are representative examples: "You must be impartial and listen to high and low alike" (1:17); "You shall not covet" (5:21); "Do not be hard-hearted or close-fisted with your countryman in his need" (15:7); "See that you do not harbour iniquitous thoughts" (15:19); "Be generous . . . because the Lord your God has blessed you" (15:14). These are not laws, which may be kept or broken, but a preacher's exhortations designed to inculcate moral norms and encourage a pattern of behavior that would be distinctly Israelite. They are nonenforceable obligations and expectations, the moral conventions that undergird society. But they stem from a firm belief in the worth of the individual and the value of human relationships. "To read the Deuteronomic law is to feel oneself living with a closely-knit, brotherly, godly and civilised society, however far the vision was from the reality."[5]

This emphasis on the significance of the spiritual is well expressed by the French priest Michael Quoist:

> If all had enough to eat, a roof over their heads, a car, a refrigerator . . . , if all had a decent education and a profession or trade . . . , if science and technology had gained mastery of nature, medicine had conquered all diseases . . . , if the politi-

5. G. R. Dunstan, *The Artifice of Ethics* (London: SCM, 1974), p. 24.

84

cal and economic institutions of society were equally just to all, would the earth be a paradise of unalloyed happiness? No, not if the heart of man remained unchanged. You must strive in every way to make contemporary society a place where a truly human life can be lived, but you must at the same time guard against falling into the illusion that social reform, of itself, can guarantee man's salvation. What should you start with then — man and his attitudes, or society and its institutions? Seek to change them both simultaneously. But don't forget that, in the end, it is man who must be transformed for it is man's salvation which is at stake. Evil has made such inroads into the life of man that no man can even begin to root it out without the help of God. The world stands in need of the Christian.[6]

The authors of Deuteronomy would have said Amen to all that — except the last sentence.

So Deuteronomy speaks of a good life in the land, shared by humans, under God. The actual laws belong to a certain time and place, and to a certain type of society. Try as we may, we are not likely to find many of them realistic in our situation. We search to no avail for an economic system relevant to our age. Our local bank would have little time for a law that restricted the charging of interest on loans. You, I presume, would not take very seriously the recommendation that "no woman shall wear an article of man's clothing, nor shall a man put on a woman's dress" (22:5). We look in vain for a marginal note on trouser suits and kilts. No, many of the laws themselves are not particularly meaningful. The real point of the biblical message lies beyond them. It directs us to the realm of faith. It points to the life of the spirit, to the heart of man, and to the mind of God.

6. Michael Quoist, *The Christian Response* (Dublin: Gill and Son, 1967), p. 143.

The Blood of the Martyr

Again, seven brothers with their mother had been arrested, and were being tortured by the king with whips and thongs to force them to eat pork, when one of them, speaking for all, said: "What do you expect to learn by interrogating us? We are ready to die rather than break the laws of our fathers." The king was enraged and ordered great pans and cauldrons to be heated up, and this was done at once. Then he gave orders that the spokesman's tongue should be cut out and that he should be scalped and mutilated before the eyes of his mother and his six brothers. This wreck of a man the king ordered to be taken, still breathing, to the fire and roasted in one of the pans. As the smoke from it streamed out far and wide, the mother and her sons encouraged each other to die nobly. "The Lord God is watching," they said, "and without doubt has compassion on us. Did not Moses tell Israel to their faces in the song denouncing apostasy: 'He will have compassion on his servants'?"

. . . After the first brother had died in this way, the second was subjected to the same brutality. The skin and hair of his head were torn off, and he was asked: "Will you eat, before we tear you limb from limb?" He replied in his native language,

"Never!", and so he in turn underwent the torture. . . . After him the third was tortured. When the question was put to him, he at once showed his tongue, boldly held out his hands, and said courageously: "The God of heaven gave me these. His laws mean far more to me than they do, and it is from him that I trust to receive them back." . . . When he too was dead, they tortured the fourth in the same cruel way. . . . Then the fifth was dragged forward for torture. . . . Next the sixth was brought and said with his dying breath: "Do not delude yourself. It is our own fault that we suffer these things; we have sinned against our God and brought these appalling disasters upon ourselves. But do not suppose you will escape the consequences of trying to fight against God."

. . . The mother was the most remarkable of all, and deserves to be remembered with special honour. She watched her seven sons all die in the space of a single day, yet she bore it bravely because she put her trust in the Lord. She encouraged each in turn in her native language. Filled with noble resolution, her woman's thoughts fired by a manly spirit, she said to them: "You appeared in my womb, I know not how; it was not I who gave you life and breath and set in order your bodily frames. It is the Creator of the universe who moulds man at his birth and plans the origin of all things. Therefore he, in his mercy, will give you back life and breath again, since now you put his laws above all thought of self."

2 Maccabees 7:1-23

I HOPE THAT THE CHOICE OF A STORY from the Apocrypha will not upset you unduly. If you are a disciple of Calvin you will quickly dismiss the Second Book of Maccabees as a string of myths and stories, and you will commend the Jews for excluding it from the canon of scripture. If on the other hand you take the occasional admiring glance towards the See of Rome, you will be happy to endorse the Council of Trent's verdict on the Apocrypha, given in 1546, to the effect that "if anyone does not receive these books in their entirety as sacred and canonical, let him be anathema." Encouraged by such a positive stand-point, you will delight in finding here the scriptural warrant for keeping All Souls Day and for asking St. George to pray for England. But if you are plain Anglicans there is just a chance that you will heed the advice given by your fathers in the faith when they suggest in the sixth of the Thirty-nine Articles of Religion that the Apocrypha be read only "for example of life and instruction of manners."

Now there may not be much in 2 Maccabees 7 that will instruct us in "manners," but it does contain a powerful "example of life." For over two thousand years the history of the Jews has been one of martyrdom. In the story of the mother and her seven sons we see the genesis of that martyrdom at about 170 BC. The instigator was the Greek king Antiochus Ephipanes, who, in a bid to unify his sprawling empire, had imposed Hellenistic laws and customs on his subjects. Even Jerusalem, the cradle of monotheism, was not exempt from the pernicious influence of Greek culture and religion. Many of its inhabitants adopted the ways of Hellenism without question and were prepared to aban-don the laws of their fathers for the sake of what claimed to be a more civilized and attractive lifestyle. They neglected dietary regulations, they attempted to disguise their circumcision, and they witnessed without protest the sacrifice of animals prohibited by Moses in the temple precincts. But there were some who refused to conform. They chose to forsake the city and flee into the hills, where they hoped they could practice their ancestral faith unmolested. However, their dream was short-lived, for the king's agents followed them, determined to torture them into submission. This is the context of our story.

Within a few centuries of Antiochus's attempt to extinguish Judaism, the Jews had grown accustomed to religious persecution. But in 170 BC it was new. The people of Israel had never gone through such a crisis before. There had been slavery in Egypt and exile to Babylon, but never before had their persecutors given them the choice of death or apostasy. When it came in the second century it was a devastating surprise. The mother and her sons open the roll of Jewish martyrs. They were pioneers in more senses than one, for not only were they the first to die for their faith, they were among the first Jews to believe in an afterlife that was worth having. Previously death had been the gate not to life but to a shadowy existence where the departed were denied access even to the presence of God. The psalmist gives voice to the desperation felt by every ancient Israelite on coming close to death:

> Dost thou work wonders for the dead?
> Shall their company rise up and praise thee?
> Will they speak of thy faithful love in the grave,
>   of thy sure help in the place of Destruction?
> Will thy wonders be known in the dark,
>   thy victories in the land of oblivion? (Ps. 88:10-12)

But the Maccabean martyrs came to a new understanding of life after death. While they were not able to think in terms of resurrection in the way that Christians could later (for whom eternal life was guaranteed because Christ had conquered death), they could have echoed Paul's words in his Letter to the Romans: "I am convinced that there is nothing in death or life, in the realm of spirits or superhuman powers, in the world as it is or in the world as it shall be, in the forces of the universe, in heights or depths — nothing in all creation that can separate us from the love of God" (8:38-39). This conviction earned for the mother and her seven sons a place in both the Jewish and the Christian martyrology.

Heroism

The author of Second Maccabees as we have it is usually referred to as the epitomist, the abbreviator, or the summarizer, for that is what he is. The original account of the Maccabean heroes was told by Jason of Cyrene in five lengthy volumes, on which our abbreviator passes the following opinion:

> These five books of Jason I shall try to summarise in a single work; for I was struck by the mass of statistics and the difficulty which the bulk of the material causes to those wishing to grasp the narratives of this history. I have tried to provide for the entertainment of those who read for pleasure, the convenience of students who must commit the facts to memory, and the profit of even the casual reader. The task which I have taken upon myself in making this summary is no easy one. It means toil and late nights, just as it is no light task for the man who plans a dinner-party and aims to satisfy his guests. (2 Macc. 2:23)

We clearly owe the epitomist a considerable debt: we have only one book to read instead of five. The Second Book of Maccabees is not meant to be a strict historical record — one must read First Maccabees for that. As the author points out in the conclusion, he has purposely mixed wine with water in order to add to the reader's pleasure (2 Macc. 15:39). The aim is to encourage the faithful Jews of his own day to stand fast by recounting the deeds of their forefathers. The epitomist writes the stories in a "poor rhetoric, that stilted jargon, which was the curse of third-rate authors in the Hellenistic world; but if you can penetrate through this repellent medium, you can still touch an anguish that was once real and quivering, and an endurance and faith that was once the supreme effort of the human soul."[1] Despite such poor style, First and Second Maccabees are commended as suitable reading for Christians by St. Augustine in *The City of God*, where he states that these books "are regarded as canonical by the Church (though not by the Jews) because of the savage, the amazing sufferings endured by some of the martyrs who, before Christ's coming in his human body, contended even unto death for the cause of God's Law, and held firm under the most appalling agonies."[2] As a result, the mother and her seven sons found a place in the Christian calendar, and though their memorial has been removed from the Roman Catholic list of saints' days, they are still recognized by the Orthodox, who commemorate their martyrdom on August 1.

The root meaning of the word *martyr* is "witness." Martyrs point beyond themselves to God. They testify through pain and isolation to what they believe to be true. Even though the chips are down, they refuse to compromise their beliefs; they are witnesses unto death. Their response to the gospel is the ultimate response. But what value does meditating on the role of the martyr have for us? To what end do we keep so many red-letter days? Principally because the martyrs remind us of the heroic side of Christianity. Many people feel a longing to serve some major cause. They have an urge to sacrifice, to give themselves unreservedly to something worthwhile. If they consider the cause to be great enough, they will lay down their

1. E. Bevan, *Jerusalem under the High-Priests* (London: Arnold, 1958), p. 83.

2. Augustine, *The City of God*, book 18, ch. 36, trans. H. Bettenson, Penguin Classics Series (Harmondsworth, Middlesex, 1972), pp. 810f.

lives for it. Such a cause can be either secular or religious. In the winter of 1969 a young student named Jan Palach sat in the main square in Prague and set himself afire. He was protesting the Russian invasion of his country, and he obviously felt that the ensuing loss of freedom called from him the supreme sacrifice as a form of protest. Archbishop Romero, in the name of Christ, condemned tyranny, greed, and violence in Latin America, knowing full well that sooner or later he would pay for such outspokenness with his life. He died in a hail of bullets as he stood at the altar in his own cathedral.

We admire such heroism, and in our better moments wish we could emulate it, not perhaps to the same degree, but we would like to be able to go some of the way. The bugle call thrills us and awakens our passion. We wish that we too had the courage to stand up and be counted, whatever the consequences; that we too could articulate our concern for some worthwhile cause regardless of the outcome. The vast majority of us, however, do not give in to that secret longing. We find all kinds of reasons why we cannot do what we would like to see ourselves doing. While the bugle thrills us, it also frightens us. It frightens us because it calls us away from much that we hold dear, away from the security bestowed by the familiar. It bids us venture into uncharted waters. Our greatest wish is to be adventurers, but when the crunch comes we retreat.

Baron Von Hugel discusses this conflict experienced by so many people, and calls it the tension between the "homely and the heroic." This tension is felt especially by young idealists. It also is recognizable in the history of the Church. From the earliest times there have been those who have wanted to make the life of faith rigorous and demanding. They have sought to make the path of discipleship arduous and difficult. They have tried to heighten the Christian standard, making it exclusive and severe. Others have wanted to lower the standard, and make things easier for Christ's followers. They have sought to ensure that common clay like us can have a recognized place in the household of faith.

As a rule, Anglicans are rarely too heroic. They are not remembered for their efforts in making the practice of religion more difficult for the faithful. If anything they have erred by being too homely. They have been accused of creating a version of Christianity that is too soft and comfortable, a faith that makes no great demands, a faith from which the heroic element, the dangerous element, has been removed. At least, their ideas are often interpreted as such. If we feel that our experience of Anglicanism corroborates this, we need to set firmly within our sights that side of the Christian religion that we are prone to neglect. When we do contemplate the heroic dimension of the faith, we should allow ourselves to be influenced by it. We may know before we begin that such contemplation will not make martyrs of us, but it will serve to remind us that heroism always has been and always will be a mark of authentic Christianity.

Ordinary People

Accounts of martyrdom remind us that martyrs are ordinary people. The famous Danish theologian Søren Kierkegaard described Christianity as something "which a group of fishermen gave to the world." The New Testament still stands as one of the wonders of antiquity, not least because it was produced by very insignificant characters. It is the product of ordinary people and the story of ordinary people. It is true that the Emperor Augustus is in it. But he is mentioned only as a peg on which to hang the birth of Jesus. Pontius Pilate, the wily Roman governor, is in it. But he appears only in order to provide a historical reference for the crucifixion; apart from that, his contribution to the story is shameful. On a purely human level Jesus of Nazareth was in no way remarkable. He did none of the things that are a passport to success. In this context the words of the nineteenth-century American preacher Phillips Brooks, in a memorable sermon entitled *The Loser* (who won), come to mind:

> Here is a man who was born in a lowly manger, the child of a peasant woman. He grew up in an obscure village. He worked in a carpenter's shop until he was thirty, and then for three years he was an itinerant preacher. He never wrote a book. He never held an office. He never went to college. He never owned a house. He never had a family. He never travelled two hundred miles from the place where he was born. He never did one of the things that usually accompany greatness. He had no credentials but himself. He had nothing to do with this world except the power of his divine manhood. While still a young man, the tide of popular opinion turned against him. His friends ran away. One of them denied him. He was turned over to his enemies. He went through the mockery of a trial. He was nailed upon a cross between two thieves. His executioners gambled for the only piece of property he had on earth while he was dying — his coat. When he was dead, he was taken down and laid in a borrowed tomb through the pity of a friend.

Yet the followers of this "very ordinary" man were in the front line when it came to martyrdom. Because they dared voice their discontent with the status quo, they knew the pain of isolation, misunderstanding, and inner turmoil. For unwittingly they were responding to him who brings not peace but the sword. Ordinary men and women, they continued the tradition of Jewish martyrdom, a tradition described so vividly by the author of the Letter to the Hebrews. "They were tortured, they had to face jeers and flogging, even fetters and prison bars.

They were stoned, they were sawn in two, they were put to the sword, they went about dressed in skins of sheep or goats, in poverty, distress and misery. They were refugees in deserts and on the hills, hiding in caves and holes in the ground" (11:30-32). These words can just as easily be applied to the earliest Christians from Stephen onwards.

During the eighties a little pamphlet called *Voice of the Martyrs* occasionally found its way onto my desk. It was published by the Christian Mission to the Communist World. One of the aims of this organisation was to highlight the dangers and difficulties faced by Christians living in totalitarian states. Each month new names were added to the list of those imprisoned for teaching and propagating the Christian faith. The most striking thing about these modern witnesses was their ordinariness. They did not appear to have any special ability or talent. They had never hit the headlines in their own country or any other. They were not the Solzhenitzyns or Sakharovs of this world, but elders of the Pentecostal Church, Baptist pastors from eastern Siberia, priests and laity of the Orthodox Church. Those whom the Church regards as heroes are almost invariably ordinary people. Their only distinguishing mark is their faith.

I stress this point because it is easy to think, as we read the martyrology or flick through the Church's calendar, that martyrs are extraordinary people. But the history of the Church, from the first day to this, teaches us that they are not. Given a different set of circumstances they could include in their number you and me.

Creative Suffering

During the last century inhabitants of Hawaii who caught leprosy were quarantined on the island of Molokai. This was necessary because there was no cure for this dreadful disease. Since they were under sentence of death, it is not difficult to imagine the debauched state in which these people lived. Appalled by their circumstances, the local Roman Catholic bishop appealed for priests to go to Molokai. He found one volunteer, a Belgian called Joseph Damien. For twelve years Father Damien lived with the lepers, doing what he could to relieve their pain, teaching them to live better lives, and giving them Christian burial, until one morning he spilled boiling water on his foot and realized that he felt no pain. At the age of forty-nine Damien died a leper. He was later beatified.

Maximilian Kolbe was a Franciscan priest. When the Nazis invaded his native Poland in 1939 he was the guardian at one of the order's friaries. With thousands of his fellow countrymen, Kolbe was eventually sent to a concentration camp. Mutiny among the prisoners brought reprisals from the SS. Ten men were chosen at random on the parade ground to be starved to death. One of them was the father of a young family. When Kolbe heard this he volunteered to take the man's place, and he died of enforced starvation in 1944. The person whom he saved lived to tell the tale, and a few years ago Maximilian Kolbe was canonized.

Martyrs, we said earlier, are witnesses, men and women who point beyond themselves. But why don't they stop short of death? What is the point of making the ultimate sacrifice? What good is a signpost when it has been knocked down? What value has the testimony of a dead witness? To the world the death of the martyr looks like a defeat, and inasmuch as a human life is lost, it is precisely that. But Christianity, by focusing on the life and death of Jesus, teaches that it is a creative defeat, a defeat out of which good comes. Martyrs voluntarily give up their lives to achieve a specific goal. The element of creativity, linked to the willing acceptance of certain death, may be perceived in two ways.

First, every martyrdom testifies to what has been described as "creative courage." This is courage of a peculiar kind, in that it does more than react bravely to certain circumstances. In order to achieve its goal, it creates a crisis, it forces a situation that need never have arisen. We see it in Jesus when he left Galilee for the last time and traveled southwards to Judea, knowing that he would never return home. In the expressions they use and the details they record, the evangelists depict Jesus' courageous acceptance of his destiny and underline the anxiety that the impending crisis caused his disciples. Luke states that Jesus "set his face resolutely towards Jerusalem" (9:51), while Mark, who regards Jerusalem as the real center of hostility towards leader and followers alike, adds that "the disciples were filled with awe, while those who followed behind were afraid" (10:32). Had he stayed in Galilee he could have ended his days as a respected rabbi, teacher, and healer, loved and revered by the common people. But he chose to go to Jerusalem to meet his enemies. It was not folly that prompted him to do this, but courage, the courage that leads a man to track down evil and to combat it. The death of Martin Luther King was not, strictly speaking, voluntary, but in championing the cause of black Americans, he knew it was a strong possibility. His determination to force a crisis and continue his campaign for equal rights led, eventually, to his assassination. The same courage inspired Damien and Kolbe; it created the situations in which they found themselves. It is this courage that we salute when we remember them.

Secondly, the sacrifice of the martyr is described as creative because its whole purpose is remedial. In the case of Damien and Kolbe the remedy or the good created by their suffering is obvious. Damien's dedication to the people of Molokai and his readiness to lay down his life eventually led to the establishment of a mission to lepers throughout the world. One man revolu-

tionized the Church's attitude to leprosy. Kolbe's voluntary starvation prevented a Polish family from being torn apart by evil
men. The element of creativity is not absent either from the
martyrdom of the mother and her seven sons. It was this kind
of experience that led the Jews to believe in an afterlife, an
afterlife that was not to be equated with the nebulous existence
of Sheol, the abode of the dead, but a life in which the righteous
would live with the Lord. The first Jewish martyrs voiced the
clear conviction that death was not the end. Perhaps it was this
conviction that led Tertullian, an early champion of Christian
orthodoxy, to declare that "the blood of the martyr is the seed
of the Church."

Blind Guides?

Then the disciples came to him and said, "Do you know that the Pharisees have taken great offence at what you have been saying?" His answer was: ". . . Leave them alone; they are blind guides of blind men, and if one blind man guides another they will both fall into the ditch."

Matthew 15:12-14

"Alas for you, lawyers and Pharisees, hypocrites! You pay tithes of mint and dill and cumin; but you have overlooked the weightier demands of the Law, justice, mercy and good faith. It is these you should have practised, without neglecting the others. Blind guides! You strain off a midge, yet gulp down a camel! Alas for you, lawyers and Pharisees, hypocrites! You clean the outside of the cup and dish, which you have filled inside by robbery and self-indulgence! Blind Pharisee! Clean the inside of the cup first; then the outside will be clean also. Alas for you, lawyers and Pharisees, hypocrites! You are like tombs covered with whitewash; they look well from outside, but inside they are full of dead men's bones and all kinds of filth.

*So it is with you: outside you look like honest men, but inside
you are brim-full of hypocrisy and crime. . . . You snakes, you
vipers' brood, how can you escape being condemned to hell?"*

Matthew 23:23-33

THE GOSPELS FREQUENTLY portray Jesus engaging in controversy with his contemporaries. They highlight his disagreement with the religious authorities over such matters as
keeping the Sabbath holy, eating with unwashed hands, the
authority to forgive sins, and the legality of divorce. While it
could be argued that the discussions on some of these issues
indicate nothing more than a difference in emphasis or interpretation, the repeated denunciations of Matthew 23 display a
merciless hostility on the part of Jesus towards one group of
fellow Jews, namely the Pharisees. In calling into question the
sincerity of the Jewish leadership, "hypocrites," "vipers," and
"blind guides" seem to be favorite labels. Pharisaism is a bad
system that produces bad people.

What is the Christian reader to make of such extreme
vituperation? How is Jesus' uncharacteristically vicious attack
on the Pharisees to be explained? The question may be
addressed in one of two ways: (1) by taking the view that *any*
teaching attributed to Jesus in the Gospels is authentic, in the
sense that it was actually given by him, or (2) by assuming that
the words were placed on Jesus' lips by the evangelists writing
during the final decades of the first century AD.

Those who accept the first option insist on the "truth" of
any statement attributed to Jesus, however uncharacteristic or
unpalatable it may be. They claim that whatever he said has
abiding value for his followers and is therefore normative for
Christian belief. They assume without question that since the
Jewish leaders of his day were vilified by Jesus, they must have

deserved such treatment. In the words of one conservative scholar, "If Jesus, who was the Incarnation of God, and therefore the personification of perfect knowledge and truth, thus depicts the Pharisees, thus they must have been and not otherwise; no more is to be said."[1] Proponents of the alternative view attribute statements that they consider unworthy of Jesus, though allegedly made by him, to the evangelists. As a result, they look for specific situational factors that may have prompted expressions of enmity and hatred. Such an approach recognizes that the anti-Jewish statements in the Gospels belong not to the time of Jesus but to the latter part of the first century AD, when there was constant and open confrontation between the Church and the Synagogue. The clash between these two groups is reflected in the accounts of the disputes between Jesus and the Pharisees recorded by the evangelists. In other words, the existence of contingent factors helps to explain Jesus' strong condemnation of his contemporaries, and in consequence it could be argued that his statements carry less authority.

These two ways of regarding the words of Jesus have an immediate bearing on the description of the Pharisees given in the Gospels. Is what we read in Scripture factually true, or is every negative utterance the product of a hostile writer with an axe to grind? Was the rift between Jesus and the leaders of the Pharisaic movement as great as we are led to believe? Those steeped in the Christian tradition inevitably regard the Pharisee as the worst possible type of Jew and accept without demur what is still the standard dictionary definition: "a formal, sanctimonious, and hypocritical person." Furthermore, they deduce from the New Testament that Jesus had nothing whatever in

1. A. Lukyn Williams, *Talmudic Judaism and Christianity* (London: SPCK, 1933), p. 63.

common with this particular group of Jews. In textbook and commentary, from pulpit and podium, this negative view of Pharisaism has been propagated for centuries as authentic.

However, for several decades a small but determined group of biblical scholars have been aware of the need to assess the Pharisees with greater historical accuracy. Their research has led them to question the reliability of the account given by the evangelists and to turn to other sources in their desire to provide a more favorable and honest portrayal of the founding fathers of postbiblical Judaism. But it is doubtful whether this painstaking research has made any perceptible impact on the person in the pew, who listens to denunciations of the Pharisees on several Sundays during the Christian year, not to mention Holy Week. This essay is an attempt to bring the fruits of modern scholarship within reach of the nonspecialist by outlining the reassessment of Pharisaism currently underway in scholarly circles and by seeking to demonstrate the relevance of such reassessment for every Christian congregation.

A New Approach

One of the earliest examples of intellectual honesty among Christian biblical scholars with regard to Judaism in general, and Pharisaism in particular, is the work of the Harvard professor George Foot Moore. In a pioneering article entitled "Christian Writers on Judaism," which appeared in the *Harvard Theological Review* for 1921, Moore made a full survey of what Christians had written about Jews over the past nineteen hundred years. His findings led him to the conclusion that the vast majority of Christian theologians have taken an interest in Judaism for one reason only: to demonstrate its inferiority. He castigated his contemporaries, especially German scholars whose works were quickly becoming authoritative, for giving a false picture of Judaism in order to justify its displacement by Christianity. He accused them of portraying the Judaism of the early Christian centuries as a barren, if not moribund, religion, with which Jesus of Nazareth was at variance. He criticized them for concentrating on the New Testament at the expense of other, less prejudiced, sources. To rely solely on the Gospels for an appraisal of the Pharisees was, in his opinion, tantamount to accepting only the evidence of the Talmud or the Koran for the life and work of Jesus.

Despite Moore's criticisms, the negative attitude towards Judaism among Christian scholars persisted. His contemporaries were reluctant to change their minds, and because many of them were highly respected teachers, their influence on their pupils may be detected long after the 1920s. One example must suffice. For the past thirty-five years *The Interpreter's Dictionary of the Bible* has been a constant source of reference for teachers, preachers, students, and study-group leaders. It is to be found in most parish libraries and is an excellent source for anyone wishing to increase their knowledge of biblical subjects. The author of the article on the Pharisees is Matthew Black, a former professor at the University of St Andrew's in Scotland and a respected New Testament scholar. Black emphasizes the connection between the Pharisees of Jesus' day and the rabbis — the religious leaders of the Jews after the destruction of the Jerusalem temple in AD 70. For him the link is an excessive legalism, which robbed Judaism of its vitality and left it lifeless. "Pharisaism," he writes, "is the immediate ancestor of rabbinical (or normative) Judaism, the arid and sterile religion of the Jews after the fall of Jerusalem." To demonstrate how offensive this false description of the Pharisees is to Jewish readers, it is enough to quote the reaction of Samuel Sandmel, who was at one time provost and professor at the Hebrew Union College

— Jewish Institute of Religion, Cincinnati. He writes, "I am personally a descendant of the Rabbinic religion, the sterility of which was not so complete as to prevent my being born. Black's article is not only unreliable, it is disgraceful that it should have appeared in the same dictionary to which I and some dozen other Jews contributed."[2]

This one example could be multiplied. Unfortunately, it may be stated without equivocation that the majority of Christian scholars disregarded Moore's complaint. In their discussions of Pharisaism, they were ready to accept the testimony of the Gospels without questioning its validity. They did not entertain the possibility that the evangelists were biased and therefore deliberately attempting to discredit the Jewish leadership. Furthermore, they neglected non-Christian sources that, though belonging to the New Testament period, provide a very different picture of the nature of Pharisaism.

However, Moore was not entirely without support. Not only did Jewish scholars corroborate his findings, but also Christian students of Judaism began to take his views seriously. One of the first to do so was the Anglican clergyman James W. Parkes, who wrote voluminously almost up to his death in 1982 in defense of the Pharisees and their religion. The eminent biblical scholar W. D. Davies, formerly of Duke University, concluded a lecture on the Pharisees delivered in Wales in 1954 by saying that "a reassessment of Pharisaism and new appreciation of it among Christians should become a prime necessity."[3] In the 1970s and 1980s notable contributions to the debate were made by Roman Catholic scholars in an attempt to put into practice the recommendations made in 1965 by the

2. Samuel Sandmel, *The First Christian Century in Judaism and Christianity: Certainties and Uncertainties* (New York: Oxford University Press, 1969), p. 101.
3. W. D. Davies, *Introduction to Pharisaism* (Philadelphia: Fortress Press, 1967), p. 28.

Second Vatican Council with reference to fostering better relations between the Church of Rome and peoples of other faiths. Among them the name of John Pawlikowski, a Chicago professor, comes to the fore. Several books by this prolific scholar contain chapters that assess the contribution of the Pharisees in an objective and unbiased manner.[4]

The first step in the process of reassessment is to consider the nature and significance of the sources from which we derive our knowledge of Pharisaism. There are three: the New Testament, the rabbinic traditions of the first two centuries AD, and the writings of the first-century Jewish historian Josephus. Although these sources provide unequivocal testimony to the existence of the Pharisees as an influential group within Judaism, they are beset by one major difficulty: they fail to agree with one another. When discussing the nature of Pharisaism, they all reach different conclusions. To make matters worse, there is disagreement even within the same source. One way of dealing with the differences between the sources is by recognizing that each one has its own emphasis, for it is only when that emphasis is properly appreciated that a true and clear picture of Pharisaism will emerge. Before the historian can describe the movement, the biblical commentator must come to grips with the text and its context. One must ask: What does the writer of any particular source seek to achieve by mentioning the Pharisees? How does his portrayal of them support his point of view?

Let us turn briefly to the sources themselves, starting with the New Testament but confining ourselves to the Gospels. Although the evangelists portray the Pharisees in a bad light

---

4. John Pawlikowski, *Catechetics and Prejudice* (New York: Paulist, 1973); *Sinai and Calvary: Meeting of Two Peoples* (Beverly Hills: Benziger, 1976); *Jesus and the Theology of Israel* (Wilmington: Glazier, 1989).

most of the time, we should not lose sight of some positive references. Luke, for example, states that Pharisees invited Jesus into their homes to eat with them (7:36; 11:37; 14:1), and on one occasion they warned him that Herod was out to kill him (13:31). But these are exceptions. The charge of hypocrisy and spiritual blindness made in Matthew 15 and the seven "woes" ("alas" in modern translations) of Matthew 23, which introduce the most malicious blanket condemnations, are much more typical of the attitude expressed by the biblical authors.

As we have already pointed out, for those who take a literalist view of the Bible, the fact that these negative descriptions are ascribed to Jesus makes them factually correct. In their opinion there is no need to turn to other sources for information about the Pharisees; an inerrant and inspired Scripture suffices. But biblical critics adopt a different approach. Because they regard the New Testament as "the Word of God in the words of men," they do not believe that its contents are entirely without bias, and therefore free of prejudice when describing those who opposed Christianity. They also stress that the authors were primarily theologians, not historians, whose intention was to preach the risen Christ and defend the faith rather than recount first-century history. Furthermore, they recognize and take account of contingent situational factors in any assessment of the evidence. They trace the animosity not to Jesus but to the evangelists, because they believe that it stems from a time when Jew and Christian were at loggerheads. They cannot, therefore, accept that the New Testament portrait of the Pharisee is a correct one. An example of this viewpoint is found in the work of the British New Testament scholar N. T. Wright, the dean of Lichfield Cathedral, who concludes that in this case the testimony of the Bible is unreliable. He writes: "It is very difficult to use the New Testament as basic material in our reconstruction of the Pharisees."[5]

There are at least three contingent factors that may account for the emergence of hostile Christian literature composed during the final decades of the first century. The first is the expulsion of Christians from the synagogues (John 9:34; 16:2). The hostility of the evangelists could be a reaction to Jewish persecution, which in turn was fuelled by the attempts of Jesus' followers to break away from Judaism by claiming that they constituted a movement apart from the Synagogue. The second is that Pharisaism proved to be a threat to Christianity because it demonstrated that, despite the fall of the temple, the Jewish religion was very much alive and able to compete for the souls of pagans. In order to marginalize Judaism and persuade their readers that it was no longer a viable option, the evangelists made every effort to discredit the leaders. They portray them as the sworn enemies of Jesus and deserving of his criticisms. Finally, the authors of the New Testament were ever mindful of the power of the Roman Empire and took great pains not to kindle its wrath. For they knew that if the Christian Church was to succeed in its mission, the support of Rome was essential. One way of earning the favor of the empire was to show that the chief opponents of Jesus were Jews, not Romans; that it was his own people, not a foreign power, who crucified him.

Just as the Christian turns instinctively to the New Testament to learn about the Pharisees, the Jew turns to rabbinical literature. Here, as one would expect, the picture is very different. Although the rabbis of a later generation hardly ever refer to the political stance of the Pharisees against the Greeks and the Romans, they take great interest in their spirituality

5. N. T. Wright, *The New Testament and the People of God* (London: SPCK, 1992), p. 184.

because they regard them as the saviors of Judaism in times of crisis. They admire them for the very reason that earned them the condemnation of the evangelists, namely faithful adherence to the Law. But the most prominent characteristics of this highly respected group are godliness, learning, compassion, and brotherly love. For the Pharisee, the ultimate standard in personal relationships was the golden rule. Even so, rabbinical literature is not blind to the shortcomings of the Pharisees. The Talmud, the great compendium of Jewish practices and beliefs produced around AD 500, records the Pharisees' own verdict on themselves. They are just as ready as Jesus to criticize ostentation in matters of faith. Those who make a public show of their religion, but nurture deceit in their hearts, are condemned unsparingly. The bickering and the difference of opinion within the movement are also recorded. But the fact that some Pharisees were hypocritical and quarrelsome does not justify the wholesale charges brought against them in Matthew 23. If Jesus was a true teacher, surely he must be acquitted of such hasty generalizations.

Our final source is the work of Josephus, a commander of the Jewish forces in the nation's rebellion against the Romans in AD 66-73. Early in the war he was taken prisoner, and he spent the rest of his life in Rome, where he died at the turn of the century. His writings are important in our quest for the true picture of the Pharisees for three reasons. The first is that he wrote as a historian, not a theologian. Unlike the evangelists and the rabbis, he had no ulterior motive; he wished only to record facts. The second is that he was an eyewitness of the events that he records and is therefore likely to have given a correct account of them. Finally, his works were not, in all probability, rewritten or edited by others after him, as those of the evangelists and the rabbis were. In this source, the period and the account given of it correspond.

Josephus refers frequently to the Pharisees as the most prominent group among the Jews from the second century BC onwards. During periods of oppression and persecution they uphold the rights of the Jews. They emerge as champions of their people during crucial moments in their history: the time of the Maccabees, the reign of Herod, the first decade of the Christian era when Judea became a Roman province, and during the rebellion of AD 66. Josephus suggests that they were an influential body, which the rulers would do well to heed. But in addition to having political interests, they were also religious leaders. They were noted for their loyalty to God, their strict adherence to the Law of Moses, and their emphasis on social justice, compassion, and tolerance. However, Josephus did not like the Pharisees. For personal reasons he objected to their political power and failed to see why their interpretation of the Law should be paramount.

These, then, are the main sources of our knowledge of the Pharisees during the time of Jesus. The fact that each of them has its own agenda makes scholars reluctant to accept their evidence without demur. But however subjective the descriptions may be, taken together they provide a portrait of the Pharisees that is accepted as being historically accurate. It is possible to pinpoint four characteristics. The first is their piety; they were observant Jews determined to keep God's Law. All three sources agree on this. The second is their influence among the ordinary people. Josephus makes much of this point, but it is mentioned in the other sources as well. The third is their political power. Though this is not mentioned by the rabbis, and only hinted at in the Gospels, it features prominently in Josephus. Finally, their hypocrisy. The rabbis and Josephus note this, but the New Testament highlights it and applies it indiscriminately to all members of the group.

Achievements

The Pharisees first appeared during the second century BC, when Judas Maccabeus led his fellow Jews in a revolt against their Greek overlords. If the people of Judah were to resist the attractions of paganism, they needed strong religious leaders. A corrupt priesthood had embraced the Greek way of life, and almost overnight it lost all prestige. The Second Book of Maccabees relates in graphic detail how Jason, brother of Onias, "who had obtained the high priesthood by corrupt means," became totally immersed in Greek culture.

> He abolished the lawful way of life and introduced practices which were against the law. He lost no time in establishing a sports-stadium at the foot of the citadel itself, and he made the most outstanding of the young men assume the Greek athlete's hat. So Hellenism reached a high point with the introduction of foreign customs through the boundless wickedness of the impious Jason. As a result, the priests no longer had any enthusiasm for their duties at the altar, but despised the temple and neglected the sacrifices; and in defiance of the law they eagerly contributed to the expenses of the wrestling-school whenever the opening gong called them. They placed no value on their hereditary dignities, but cared above everything for Hellenic honours. (2 Macc. 4:12-15)

Though the priests were nominally the nation's religious leaders, in the face of such corruption the Pharisees assumed the authority to make decisions in matters of faith and morals. These new lay leaders realized that in order to survive the threats posed by its opponents, traditional Judaism had to adapt to the situation in which it found itself. In their attempt to save their ancestral faith, they emphasized the moral and ritual principles enshrined in the Law and strove to make them applicable to the daily life of every Jew.

In stressing public and private morality, the Pharisees were worthy successors of Moses and the great prophets of Israel. Ever since the covenant was made on Mount Sinai between God and his people, the ethical obligations of the Law had been of paramount importance to the religious leaders. But a glance at the history of Israel will demonstrate that the nation had consistently failed to keep the commandments. Although the ritual laws governing sacrifices and offerings were observed, the righteousness and justice demanded by God were entirely lacking; hence the fierce denunciations of Amos, Hosea, and Micah.

> Listen, you leaders of Jacob, rulers of Israel,
> should you not know what is right?
> You hate good and love evil,
> you flay men alive and tear the very flesh from their bones;
> you devour the flesh of my people,
> strip off their skin, splinter their bones;
> you shred them like flesh into a pot,
> like meat into a cauldron.
> Then they will call to the Lord, and he will give them no
> answer. (Mic. 3:1-4)

The Pharisees insisted that in order to avoid the catastrophe predicted by these eighth-century prophets, the Jews had to take the commandments seriously. If it was to survive, Judaism had to undergo a transformation based on adherence to every detail of the Law, moral and ritual. The Sinai covenant must be the basis of life for the individual and society.

But if the commandments were to be kept, they had to be applied to everyday life in a realistic way and their relevance to the ordinary Jew demonstrated. The inability of the prophets to convince Israel of the need to repent convinced the Pharisees of the need for a new strategy. In their view, God's illustrious envoys had failed because the content of their preaching was too vague. A message expressed in such general terms as "Let justice roll on like a river, and righteousness like an ever-flowing stream" (Amos 5:24) was far too imprecise. The same criticism could be made of the Law of Moses. How did people actually "love" their neighbors? What was meant by "honoring" one's parents? How was the Sabbath to be kept as a day of rest on which "any work" was forbidden on pain of death? How did one love God with all one's heart, soul, and strength?

But the lack of precision was not the only problem. It was obvious from such books as Exodus and Deuteronomy that very many Old Testament laws were irrelevant for a second century BC Jew. Much of the legislation recorded in the Five Books was far more suited to farmers than to townspeople and to priests rather than laity. During the early period of the nation's history, when Israel was basically an agricultural society, these laws could be observed with but little attempt at adaptation. But when, under the impact of Greek civilization, the Jew became a city dweller, the inadequacy of the Law of Moses became apparent. How were the Jewish communities in Alexandria, Athens, and Rome to preserve their distinctive lifestyle and practice their religion in an environment that was not only pagan but urban, if their only law code was intended for an agrarian society? The Law was certainly a help, but it did not by any means cover every eventuality. It is true that through the ministry of the priest it could assure the individual of forgiveness and atonement. But the promise of large flocks, fruitful fields, and full barns as a reward for good living, though relevant once, meant little to a shopkeeper in Antioch or a tailor in Corinth.

To make God's commandments applicable, the Pharisees developed the concept of a dual Law, or to use the Hebrew term, a dual Torah: written and oral. The former corresponded to the first section of our modern Bible, which is traditionally ascribed to Moses and known as the Five Books. The latter fully came into operation only just before the time of Christ, though it too, according to Jewish tradition, could be traced to Moses. Because of its ancient origin, the oral Law was therefore just as authoritative as the written Law. It is referred to in the various translations of the New Testament as "the tradition of the elders," "the teaching handed down by our ancestors," and "an old-established tradition" (Matt. 15:2; Mk 7:3). In some ways it is comparable to the concept of "tradition" in Roman Catholicism, namely the authoritative interpretation of Scripture that has evolved over the centuries.

Because the Pharisees believed that the written Law was far too imprecise to be of any practical use, they adapted ancient statutes and ordinances to meet the challenge of a new age; the moral principles of the covenant expressed in the written Law were applied realistically to the daily life of the urban Jew. This meant spelling out in detail the demands of the covenant and demonstrating that keeping them to the letter was not beyond the capabilities of any individual. The written Law did not refer in so many words to such specific duties as welcoming strangers, visiting the sick, giving alms anonymously, and working for the good of society. But for the Pharisees, these and a host of other religious duties were implicit within the Five Books and incumbent upon all Jews. The same interpretative method was applied to the principle of retaliation as expressed in the oft-quoted verses from Exodus 21: "Whenever hurt is done, you shall give life for life, eye for eye, tooth for tooth, hand for hand, foot for foot, burn for burn, bruise for bruise, wound for wound." Taken literally, this would mean that anyone who struck out another person's eye or tooth would lose one of his or her own. But the Pharisees were not content with this interpretation, for the assailant might be a one-eyed person, in which case the punishment, namely blindness, would far exceed the crime. In their view, the written Law should not be taken literally in this case but interpreted in terms of compensation. The meaning of "eye for eye" was that the victim should receive the *value* of an eye, that is, realistic compensation for the harm done. Little wonder that Josephus claimed that the Pharisees tended to be lenient in administering punishment.

The development of the oral Law had far-reaching consequences for Judaism. We shall note three of them. In the first place, greater emphasis was placed on the individual. It is true that the Bible recognized the value of every person in the eyes of God. But the Pharisees went much further than the biblical authors, for they rejected the concept that the individual could be saved only through the mediation of a priest and the ritual of the temple. They dispensed with the need for a mediator by stressing that every Jew could communicate directly with God through keeping the oral Law. It was as a result of this emphasis on a personal relationship with the divine that the concept of the fatherhood of God developed in Judaism. It was through Pharisaism that the picture of God as a loving father, not only of the Jew but also of every other member of the human race, came into the New Testament. In essence, the Christian's "Our Father" is a Pharisaic prayer. It is also possible to link the Pharisees' belief in resurrection to their emphasis on the importance of the individual.

Secondly, the synagogue was given much greater prominence as a religious center alongside the temple. Although daily services were held in the synagogue, it was far more than a house of prayer. The various activities associated with it reflected the Pharisees' belief that worship was of no value unless it was linked to study and social action. Prayer was pointless if it was not informed by constant study of the Law. Piety was meaningless if charity was lacking. Hence, in addition to being a place of worship, the synagogue was a school, a library, a social center, and a court of law. It was the hub of every local Jewish community. Strangers were offered hospitality within its walls and the poor fed at its doors. In time the majority of Jews were able to dispense with the temple because they were persuaded that it was not through ritual but through study that salvation was obtained. Religious authority was henceforth in the hands of scholars, laymen proficient in the Law, not priests. The task of the teacher was to expound the written Law and apply it to the situation of each individual. The synagogue enabled every Jew to comprehend the commandments and accept the responsibility for keeping them.

Thirdly, the home and the family began to play a prominent part within the religious life of the nation. The hearth took the place of the temple, and ordinary meals replaced sacrifices. As the numerous references to purity in the New Testament illustrate, the Pharisees placed great emphasis on food. They produced numerous regulations about what to eat and how to prepare it. Some scholars see this "table-fellowship" as the hallmark of Pharisaism. It was not some ambitious political program that enabled Jews to live out their religious beliefs, but the sanctification of everyday life, symbolized by the fellowship of the dinner table. By transferring the practice of ritual purity from the sanctuary to the kitchen and the dining room, the Pharisees gave ordinary people the ability to live in accordance with the Law in their own houses without the services of a priestly mediator. This new approach to religion was prompted by the current situation in Judah. In the face of corruption in every facet of the nation's life — in its culture, its politics, and its religion — the Pharisees emphasized family life. If the attainment of national purity was beyond them, personal purity was not. It was in the homes and the synagogues of Palestine that the rebellion against oppression eventually took root. Although the Jews failed in their bid to end the Roman occupation of their country, Judaism survived the catastrophe of AD 70 because of the faith of its adherents, a faith that was nurtured by pious families in their own homes — thanks to the oral Law of the Pharisees.

Jesus and the Pharisees

It is now recognized that Jesus of Nazareth remained faithful to Judaism throughout his life. Some modern scholars have associated him with one of the many groups or parties representative of the religion of his day. The Zealots, who were in constant conflict with Rome, the Essenes, the community that is believed to be responsible for producing the Dead Sea Scrolls, the Sadducees, who were in charge of the temple and its ritual, have all been named as the possible background of Jesus' ministry. While these suggestions have not been taken too seriously, the belief that Jesus had close links with the Pharisees has generated much interest and found considerable support, especially among Jewish scholars. One of the first to put forward this theory was Joseph Klausner, a professor at the Hebrew University in Jerusalem. Writing in 1925, he claimed that "even to the last, Jesus remained a true Pharisaic Jew."[6] Forty years later Martin Buber, Paul Winter, and Asher Finkel came to the same conclusion.[7] Among the increasing number of Christians

6. Joseph Klausner, *Jesus of Nazareth* (London: Allen and Unwin, 1925), p. 319.

7. M. Buber, *Two Types of Faith* (New York: Routledge & Kegan Paul, 1961), p. 137; P. Winter, *On the Trial of Jesus* (Berlin: de Gruyter, 1962, 1974), p. 133; A. Finkel, *The Pharisees and the Teacher of Nazareth* (Leiden: Brill, 1964), passim.

drawn to this view is W. E. Phipps, who describes Jesus as a "prophetic Pharisee."[8]

Despite scholarly opinion, many Christians have difficulty in believing that Jesus had anything in common with the Pharisees. Does not the New Testament emphasize the irreconcilable differences between him and this group's interpretation of Judaism? However, now that a fuller and more balanced picture of Pharisaism has emerged, it is not inappropriate to consider the similarities between the teaching of Jesus and that of this influential movement. There is a striking correspondence between the Pharisees' characteristics noted above and Jesus' teachings. The Gospels refer frequently to the value of the individual. If even a sparrow does not fall to the ground without God knowing, how much more important is a human being. "As for you, even the hairs of your head have all been counted. So have no fear; you are worth more than any number of sparrows" (Matt. 10:30-31). Jesus' concept of the fatherhood of God may well go far beyond that of the Pharisees, nevertheless his teaching echoes one of their basic concepts; Jesus was not the first to emphasize the close relationship between God and human beings. Jesus' ministry of teaching, preaching, and healing, often carried out in synagogues, points to an affinity with early rabbis. As has been already pointed out, Jesus ate with Pharisees, and some claim that the Last Supper was a "fellowship meal" like those partaken of in Pharisaic circles. The early Christian teaching of resurrection can be traced to Jesus, and beyond him to the Pharisees. When Jesus was asked by a Pharisee which was the greatest commandment in the Law, he replied, "'Love the Lord your God with all your heart, with all your soul, with all your mind.' That is the greatest com-

8. W. E. Phipps, "Jesus, the Prophetic Pharisee," *Journal of Ecumenical Studies* 14 (1977): pp. 17-31.

mandment. It comes first. The second is like it: 'Love your neighbour as yourself.' Everything in the Law and the prophets hangs on these two commandments" (Matt. 22:37-40). The Pharisee who asked the question would have been delighted with the answer. For Jesus, as for the Pharisees, the golden rule, "Treat others as you would like them to treat you" (Luke 6:31), is of paramount importance. A detailed and unbiased examination of such correspondences leads one respected New Testament scholar to conclude that he can "find no substantial conflict between Jesus and the Pharisees."[9] From this standpoint it could be claimed that the Gospel of Christ transformed, but did not annul, Pharisaism.

Although due weight should be given to the similarities, the differences cannot be ignored. The Gospels demonstrate that there was a fundamental disagreement between the Pharisees and Jesus on many topics: the status of women, the forgiveness of sins, the authority of the Law, association with sinners, and the concept of the kingdom of God are some of them. There was a difference of opinion even on the significance of the individual, for Jesus insisted that this element of Pharisaic teaching should be revised and expanded, as his attitude to healing on the Sabbath (Mark 3:1-6) demonstrates. For the Pharisees the sanctity of the Sabbath was one of the cornerstones of Judaism. In a pagan environment, the observance of a day of rest was one of the distinctive marks of every Jewish community. It has been said that "the Sabbath has preserved the Jews more than the Jews have preserved the Sabbath." Healing a person with a withered arm on a day of rest was contrary to the oral Law. If the sick man had been in danger of dying, there would have been no objection to Jesus' action. But in this particular case, there was no emergency. The

---

9. E. P. Sanders, *Jesus and Judaism* (London: SCM, 1985), p. 291.

Pharisees found fault with Jesus because they considered it more important to preserve one of the distinctive marks of their faith than perform a healing that could wait until the following day. In an age when Judaism's very survival was threatened by pagan influences, its leaders laid more stress on those elements that affected the community as a whole than on a matter relating to an individual. Jesus disagreed.

If the conclusion that Jesus and the Pharisees had much more in common than the Gospels indicate, how does one understand chapters like Matthew 23? Two explanations are offered, both of which have appealed to biblical scholars. The first claims that Jesus is not issuing a blanket condemnation of the movement as a whole. His criticism is aimed at a small group of Pharisees, bigoted extremists and hypocrites who would have been condemned by others of their kind as well. Like the rabbis of the Talmud, Jesus could see the shortcomings of those members who brought the movement into disrepute, and he made his feelings known. The attraction of this explanation is that it allows that there is some truth in the denunciations made by Jesus in the Gospels, while accepting also the positive picture of the group painted by Josephus. Its weakness is the lack of hard evidence. The Pharisees of the Gospels are almost invariably regarded as the Jewish leaders of the day, not as a few individuals whose behavior is untypical of the group as a whole. Furthermore, it is difficult to believe that a clash between Jesus and a number of extremists could have led to the major disruption between Church and Synagogue that took place later.

The second explanation, already mentioned in passing, is that the negative portrayal of the Pharisees is related to contingent factors; it reflects the difficult relationship between Christians and Jews during the latter half of the first century. The fact that the Pharisees were implacably opposed to the emerging

Christian community many years after the lifetime of Jesus has relevance for any consideration of the way in which they are portrayed in Christian literature. The anti-Jewish features of the Gospels are more intelligible when set against the background of first-century controversy. Referring to the disputes between Jesus and his fellow Jews recorded in the Gospel of Mark, one scholar states bluntly that "all the Marcan controversy stories, without exception, reflect dialogues between the Apostolic Church and its social environment, and are devoid of roots in the circumstances of the life of Jesus."[10] The evangelists condemned the Pharisees out of hand because it suited them to do so. Even those who do not go as far as this, because they believe that Jesus did disagree with the Pharisees at times, feel that the animosity recorded in the Gospels is greatly exaggerated.

In this context, it is instructive to note the difference between Matthew's portrayal and Mark's. In Matthew the Pharisees are the sworn enemies of Jesus, whereas in Mark, though they engage in a lively and sometimes bitter debate, they tolerate him, and at times admire him. Furthermore, Mark does not link the Pharisees with the Crucifixion. Which account is historically correct? If the theory that Mark wrote his Gospel first is accepted, then Matthew was writing at a time when the relationship between Jew and Christian was deteriorating rapidly. Many commentators therefore believe that Matthew, in company with Luke and John, expresses the hatred felt by the early Christians towards the Jewish leadership. For many this is the only acceptable explanation. Klaus Berger summarizes the point thus: "The Pharisees are, apparently, opponents of the early liberal community practice, projected back into the life of Jesus."[11]

10. Winter, p. 125.
11. Quoted by Sanders, p. 292.

Conclusion

What relevance does this reappraisal of the Pharisees and of Jesus' relationship with them have for the contemporary Christian? How, in this instance, does a fresh approach to ancient texts affect the modern Church? The answer is related both to the current dialogue between Christians and Jews and to the intellecual honesty of preachers and teachers. After centuries of persecuting Jews in the name of Christ, churches of all denominations have sought to make amends for such shameful behavior. Since 1945 the major Churches have made a determined effort to right the wrongs of the past. In countless statements and declarations, they have recognized that since Christian teaching has contributed to the negative stereotype of the Jew, it is incumbent upon them to propagate among their adherents a different image of God's ancient people. While progress has been made in many areas, the Christian's image of the Pharisee has been slow to change. This has made dialogue between Christians and Jews more difficult. For although, strictly speaking, Pharisaism came to an end as a specific movement around AD 220, its ideals have continued to dominate Judaism throughout the subsequent centuries. The three main branches of contemporary Judaism (Orthodox, Conservative, and Reform) differ on many important matters, but they are all agreed on the debt they owe to the Pharisees. Every believing Jew is the spiritual heir of these founding fathers. If, therefore, the teachings of the Pharisees are condemned out of hand, Jews are not likely to enter into religious discussions with Christians, simply because the foundation of their faith is being undermined. Christians who believe that interfaith dialogue should have a prominent place in our pluralist society must learn to appreciate the contribution made by the Pharisees to Judaism and be ready to revise their ideas accordingly.

Biblical scholars continue to address the issues raised by a study of Pharisaism and seek to appreciate the movement's standpoint and its place within Judaism. Much progress has been made. But if current research is to influence Christian thinking on a significant scale, pastors and teachers must grapple with the difficulties at a local level and be prepared to reconsider the age-old description of the Pharisees as "blind guides."

A Portrait of Jesus

They came to Capernaum, and on the Sabbath he went to synagogue and began to teach. The people were astounded at his teaching, for, unlike the doctors of the law, he taught with a note of authority. Now there was a man in the synagogue possessed by an unclean spirit. He shrieked: "What do you want with us, Jesus of Nazareth? Have you come to destroy us? I know who you are — the Holy One of God." Jesus rebuked him: "Be silent," he said, "and come out of him." And the unclean spirit threw the man into convulsions and with a loud cry left him. They were all dumbfounded and began to ask one another, "What is this? A new kind of teaching! He speaks with authority. When he gives orders, even the unclean spirits submit." The news spread rapidly, and he was soon spoken of all over the district of Galilee.

Mark 1:21-28

IN THE PAST THE GOSPEL OF MARK was regarded by Christian preachers and teachers as "the Cinderella Gospel." Like the little girl in the story, it was always the poor relation whenever it was compared to the other three, and as a result, it hardly ever featured in ancient liturgies. The reasons for its neglect were many, but we shall note only three of them.

First, Mark was criticized for being haphazard and muddled. One of his earliest reviewers, the second-century historian Papias, claims that Mark wrote down accurately what the Lord said and did, "but not in order." Because of this lack of structure, the Gospel was compared by Clement, a bishop of Rome at the end of the first century, to "a string of pearls." The pearls were the brief, self-contained stories of Jesus, snapshot scenes from his ministry, which circulated orally among the first Christians and were written down by Mark. The string was the cement provided by the evangelist to hold the stories together, the comments of Mark himself intended as editorial links to take the reader from one unit to the next. But there is no discernible chronology or orderly movement, the author jumps from one episode to another without providing context or clarification, so he was awarded no marks for presentation.

The second criticism concerns Mark's literary style, which has been found wanting. The perfectionists have charged him with writing barbarous Greek, surely a distressing verdict for any author! But there is some justification for such criticism, as the perusal of any literal English translation (such as the KJV or the RSV) of the original Greek will demonstrate. For instance, the words "and immediately" appear eight times in the first chapter alone. Though this breathless, repetitive style is not the kind advocated in creative writing classes, in Mark's defense one could say that the abruptness provides a sense of rapid action, presenting a portrait of Jesus as a dynamic and forceful person who moves swiftly from one place to the next. But even if that were the intention, Mark's style of writing is not one to emulate.

124

Finally, the Gospel was regarded as inferior because of its selectivity. For Mark the story of Jesus does not begin with the birth at Bethlehem, the shepherds, and the visit of the three wise men. It is only in Matthew and Luke that the infancy narratives are to be found. Mark opens his account with the baptism of Jesus, his temptation, and the calling of the first disciples. He goes in at the deep end and says nothing about the first thirty years of Jesus' life. He is equally selective with regard to Jesus' teaching. We look in vain for the Sermon on the Mount in Mark, though Matthew considers it sufficiently important to give it three chapters (chs. 5–7). If we depended on Mark, we would never have known that the "Our Father" was part of Jesus' teaching on prayer. This is not to say that Mark reproduces *none* of Jesus' teaching — in fact, about 40 percent of his Gospel consists of just that — it is simply that he seems to report less of it than the other evangelists. Compared to Matthew and Luke, he is more selective, and for this reason his Gospel achieved less prominence in services of worship than it might have done.

So Mark has been criticized for poor composition, inelegant style, and extreme selectivity. It is hardly surprising that his Gospel was regarded as second rate. But by now such negative criticism is history, for despite his apparent failings, Mark is in favor. His rehabilitation came about as a result of a new question posed by biblical scholars during the early decades of this century. Previously, each Gospel had been judged by a simple criterion: how much it told its readers about Jesus. Predictably, Mark failed such a test miserably, for compared to Matthew's Gospel, his biography of Jesus was very patchy. But when the issue became not the contents of each Gospel but the intention of the evangelist, Mark came into his own. While it is admitted that he is not a born writer, it is now recognized that he had significant literary skills. It is also recognized that he selected his material carefully for a specific purpose. The stories may not be chronological, but they do have an order that serves the author's intention. Far from being chosen in a haphazard fashion, they reflect specific theological concerns that are apparent in Mark's portrait of Jesus.

Mark addressed his Gospel to fellow Christians, who, during a time of persecution, must have wondered if there was any good news in a dark and dangerous world. While he affirms that Jesus has come to proclaim the coming of God's Kingdom, he knows that the proclamation will not go unopposed. With the advent of Jesus a battle is waged between God and Satan, truth and falsehood. The opposition to the messiahship of Jesus is both human and demonic. It is to be found not only in the Jewish religious leaders of the day, but also in the forces of evil within creation. This conflict between Jesus and his opponents is the key to understanding the Gospel. It features prominently in two aspects of Jesus' ministry, namely teaching and healing, both of which are mentioned in the description of a specimen day spent by Jesus and four companions at Capernaum, a busy little town on the Sea of Galilee.

The Teacher

Although Mark lays great stress on the teaching activity of Jesus, he does not spell out in any significant detail what that teaching is, which is odd, given that Mark considered Jesus to be such a great teacher. A suggested explanation for this penchant to stress the activity rather than record the content is that Mark simply wants to portray Jesus as "one who cares for the community." While the term "teacher" can never adequately describe Jesus' true nature, Mark uses it to draw attention to one aspect of his ministry: by his teaching he nourishes, and thereby cares for, his followers.[1]

In describing the first day of Jesus' public ministry, the evangelist says three things about his teaching. First he mentions the place: "On the Sabbath he went to synagogue." By the beginning of the first Christian century, the synagogue had come to play a crucial role in Jewish life. "In addition to worship the building, however plain, often served as a hostel for Jewish travellers, a dining hall, a school, a place for the administration of community discipline or justice, and an assembly point for the elders."[2] The synagogue was a multipurpose institution that set the boundaries necessary for the preservation of Jewish identity in a pagan environment. While there could be only one temple, the central shrine where sacrifices were made, there were hundreds of synagogues in Palestine alone. Every locality had one.

The Sabbath service was simple, consisting of prayers, readings from Scripture, and a sermon, not unlike Anglican Morning or Evening Prayer. But there was one major difference between a synagogue and a church: the synagogue community was nonclerical, it had no professional ordained ministry. The services were taken by laymen. Any competent person could be called to preach and expound the Bible, which is why Jesus was able to open his campaign in a place of worship. The local synagogue provided him with one of the chief opportunities for spreading his message. He used the place set apart by Judaism for teaching; he did not at any time shun his own tradition. Whatever differences he may have had with some of his contemporaries, he remained a Jew to the end, as his

1. E. Best, *Mark: the Gospel as Story* (Edinburgh: T. & T. Clark, 1983), pp. 62f.

2. C. J. Roetzel, *The World that Shaped the New Testament* (London: John Knox/SCM, 1987), p. 66.

adherence to the faith of his fathers, represented here by the synagogue, testifies. The history of most Christian denominations is littered with splinter groups founded by individuals who, for one reason or another, felt compelled to part company with the parent institution. Perhaps Jesus' action in Capernaum is a salutary reminder of the potential of the local church as a center for propagating the gospel.

The second point is related to Jesus' method of teaching. Mark claims that the congregation was astonished at what he said because "unlike the doctors of the law, he taught with a note of authority." This suggests that Jesus adopted a new technique for delivering his message, which was different from that usually found among synagogue teachers. But it is not clear what Mark means by this adverse comparison of Jesus with respected teachers of the law. The usual explanation is that whereas the doctors, more often referred to as "scribes," kept quoting tradition and deriving their teaching from their predecessors, Jesus sounded like a prophet inspired by God. In other words, the collective authority of what was later to become rabbinic Judaism is contrasted with the authority of the individual. The same distinction is made in Christianity between those who quote the traditional teaching of the Church when faced with difficult questions and those who claim to be speaking with divine authority. Like an Amos or a Hosea, Jesus had a personal authority and a freshness that was independent of any particular school of thought. His own personality came to the fore.

However, in an age where the need for fraternal dialogue between religions is recognized as crucial, it is unhelpful to insist that Mark's reference to authority underlines the contrast between Jesus and his Jewish contemporaries, for this explanation only accentuates the unfavorable view of Judaism espoused by Christian teachers and preachers for centuries. It must not be assumed too readily that the difference between Jesus and other Jewish teachers of his day was as pronounced as Mark suggests. After all, he was often called "teacher" (albeit more often by Mark than by Matthew and Luke), and much of his teaching is very similar to that of the rabbis in both style and content. It has therefore been suggested that Jesus acted as though he were an official rabbi who was entitled to make fresh rules of binding force. Such rabbis, who normally stayed in Judea, seldom visiting Galilee, traced their authority to Moses by means of ordination through the laying on of hands. The scribes, or doctors of the law, possessed no such authority. They were no more than elementary instructors in Scripture, who were not permitted to introduce new doctrines or make new decisions. The contrast between such people and an officially ordained rabbi would have been marked.

Although we do not know whether or not Jesus trained formally to be a rabbi, this may be the correct explanation of the perplexing reference to his authority. But it is equally possible that Mark simply wants to show that Jesus' teaching has divine approval. The point has already been made in the opening verse of the chapter that Jesus is the Son of God. Now Mark wants his readers to "see that when Jesus began his public ministry, his hearers, although they did not penetrate to the true character of his authority, could not help being made aware of its presence and contrasting it with even the highest authority they knew among human teachers."[3]

We come thirdly to the effect the teaching had on all who heard it. While Jesus' authority could lie in his prophetic personality, in his status as an ordained rabbi, or in Mark's desire to demonstrate that he was divine, the effect of his words was electrifying. He spoke with a positive certainty, with the result

3. D. E. Nineham, *Saint Mark* (Harmondsworth: Penguin, 1963), p. 75.

that "the people were astounded at his teaching." Mark makes this point several times in his Gospel, but he does not tell us why Jesus' words caused such amazement. Given that his manner was authoritative, what in the contents of his teaching caused such surprise? We can but speculate. A suggestion that appeals to me is that his teaching invariably contained an invitation to do "what is normally on the far side of human capability." He issued his listeners a challenge to attempt the impossible, a challenge that was greeted with astonishment.

In his negative assessment of the doctors of the law, Mark prepares his readers for the conflict between Jesus and the religious authorities that was soon to follow. The mention of the synagogue is significant because of its symbolism. This is the place where legal decisions were taken and trials held. Here, as in the temple, Jesus was that much more vulnerable because his opponents were on home ground. As the narrative unfolds, the conflict becomes progressively more intense; it is not resolved until the end of the story when it comes to a climax in Jesus' Crucifixion. Confrontation between Jesus and the authorities must be regarded as a central theme of Mark. It begins on the first day of Jesus' public ministry and is linked throughout the Gospel to his activities as a teacher.

The Healer

Mark reports more miraculous events than any other evangelist. In his Gospel he records eighteen miracles, chosen out of a far larger number that was available to him. Thirteen of them are miracles of healing, namely restorations and exorcisms. In the first chapter he lays particular emphasis on the latter when he deliberately draws attention to the fact that Jesus went through Galilee healing demonically induced illness, or in biblical language, "casting out devils" (1:34, 39). The perceived link in the ancient Jewish mind between demonic activity and any kind of illness is clearly illustrated in the Book of Tobit, which was written probably in the second century BC and is now included in the Apocrypha. Tobit's blindness, caused by sparrow droppings, could not be reversed by physicians, but was eventually cured by applying the entrails of a fish, the method used to drive out demons. When Tobias, Tobit's son, enquired of his guardian angel about the medicinal value of a fish's heart, liver, and gall, he was told, "You can use the heart and liver as a fumigation for any man or woman attacked by a demon or evil spirit; the attack will cease and will give no further trouble. The gall is for anointing a man's eyes when white patches have spread over them; . . . the eyes will then recover" (Tob. 6:7-8). A more familiar example of the attribution of illness to demon possession is found in Mark 9:14-29.

The first miracle Mark chooses to record is that of the healing of the demon-possessed man in the synagogue at Capernaum. It might seem that there was nothing very significant about this aspect of Jesus' ministry, for when John wrote his Gospel he ignored it altogether, presumably because in his view exorcism was such an unremarkable feature. If the Fourth Gospel was our only record of the life of Jesus, then we would have known nothing about the healing of those believed to be possessed by evil spirits. Furthermore, Paul in his epistles does not set great store by such a method of healing. But Mark saw a special significance in exorcisms, and it is this particular aspect of Jesus' healing ministry that will be considered for the rest of this chapter.

Demons were part and parcel of the thought world of the first century AD. Evil spirits lurked everywhere to harm the unwary. They lived in waste places where their cries could sometimes be heard — hence the reference to a "howling desert." But they frequently invaded towns and cities and proved to be especially dangerous to lonely travellers, newly married couples, and young children. This is why infants needed the protection of guardian angels. These demonic powers were held responsible for the irrational and inexplicable element in life. In particular, they were regarded as the cause of every kind of derangement or instability. Such was the perceived power of demons to cause mental illness that ancient peoples would go to great lengths to be delivered of them.

In some early European burial grounds archaeologists have discovered evidence of the surgical procedure known as trepanning the skull. In modern medicine this is an operation in which a small part of the skull is removed in order to relieve pressure caused by a clot or a tumor. But the holes made by the ancient surgeons were apparently too small to provide relief from any known malady. The usual explanation given for their existence is that they were made to release a demon. The disc of bone that had been removed was then worn by the patient as an amulet to prevent the evil spirit from returning. That the hole was drilled when the patient was alive is evidenced by the fact that in every case the bone had started to grow back over the cavity. Without the benefit of anesthesia such an operation must have been excruciatingly painful, but the fear of demonic possession was a powerful incentive to endure it.

Given the destructive power that demons were thought to possess, and the fact that people believed that their destiny was dictated by factors beyond their control or comprehension, it is not surprising that exorcism was very common in the ancient world. Many Jews were celebrated exorcists. One chief priest, named Sceva, had no less than seven sons, all of whom practiced exorcism (Acts 19:23ff.). Jesus, therefore, was only one among the many Jewish holy men of the time who acted as healers and exorcists. The miracle stories recorded of him are part and parcel of first century AD Jewish experience. But while Judaism practiced and sanctioned exorcism, Christianity gained supremacy over other religions during the first century because it succeeded in banishing the fear of demons. In the words of the famous historian of Christian origins, Adolph Harnack, "It was as exorcisers that Christians went out into the great world, and exorcism formed one very powerful method of their mission and propaganda."[4]

But because exorcism was considered to be the only possible cure for the deranged, there was no shortage of sorcerers and charlatans who plied a lucrative trade. These shady practitioners of magical arts used mysterious techniques and strange paraphernalia in their attempts to conquer the demons. Josephus, the first century AD Jewish historian, relates how a contemporary of his employed a method of exorcism partly attributed to Solomon:

> I have seen a fellow-countryman called Eleasar releasing people possessed by demons in the presence of Vespasian [the Roman commander in Palestine], his sons, his captains and his whole army. The cure was performed thus. He put a ring, which had under its seal one of the roots prescribed by Solomon, to the nostrils of the demoniac, and then, as the man smelled it, drew out the demon through his nostrils. When the man immediately fell down, he commanded the demon never to return to him by speaking Solomon's name and reciting the incantations which he [Solomon] had composed. When Eleasar wanted to convince the spectators that he had such power, he placed a cup or basin full of water not far away and commanded the

---

4. A. Harnack, *The Mission and Expansion of Christianity*, vol. 1 (London: Williams and Norgate, 1908), p. 152.

demon, as it left the man, to overturn it, thereby letting the spectators know that he had departed.[5]

The methods employed by such exorcists as Eleasar were often suspect, with the result that the charge of sorcery was by no means uncommon.

Jesus was part of this world of demon possession, exorcism, holy men, and charlatans. Sine he was fully human, he presumably shared the view of his contemporaries that illness, both physical and mental, was caused by Satan and his cohorts. For him, as for them, evil was immediate and real. But his method of dealing with it was quite different from that of other exorcists. He used no hocus-pocus, no abracadabra, no bizarre ritual. He simply confronted the demons and with a single authoritative word cured the sick in mind.

Mark's account contains clear evidence of the centrality of miracle and exorcism in the ministry of Jesus. In any study of the Gospel, these features must not be pushed to the periphery simply because they are incompatible with modern thinking and theologically difficult to handle. They are very much part of the story. But we may justifiably ask why Mark records so many of them. Why does he emphasize the miraculous at the expense of the teaching? One suggestion is that miracle stories made more interesting reading than sermons or wise sayings. While it may be true that for any author there was more mileage in miracles than in beatitudes, Mark's reasons are more likely to have been theological rather than pragmatic. Let us note some of them.

In company with other New Testament writers, Mark regards Christ as the power of God in action. Jesus does not materialize from thin air; his actions, especially the miracles,

5. Josephus, *The Antiquities of the Jews*, 8:2, 5.

are works that God has done through him. As Peter says in his speech to the household of Cornelius at Caesarea, "You know about Jesus of Nazareth, how God anointed him with the Holy Spirit and with power. He went about doing good and healing all who were oppressed by the devil, for God was with him" (Acts 10:38). Mark records miracles not to engender in his readers astonishment at the extraordinary feats of a wonder-worker, but in order to awaken faith in God's saving power and the coming of his kingdom mediated through Jesus. Luke and Matthew make explicit the association between the proclamation of God's kingdom and Jesus' exorcisms: "If it is by the finger of God that I drive out the devils, then be sure the kingdom of God has already come upon you" (Luke 11:20; Matt. 12:28).

Another possible reason for highlighting the miraculous is Mark's wish to show how Jesus' power manifests itself in action as well as in teaching. If he teaches "with authority," he heals "with power." This demonstration of his power to heal body and mind is part of his conflict with the Jewish religious authorities, who immediately take offense at his arrogating divine authority. The conflict even turns murderous, for as soon as the Pharisees witness Jesus healing on the Sabbath they plot with the partisans of Herod how they might do away with him (3:6). Jesus retaliates by forming a new group of twelve special companions, whom he sends out "to proclaim the Gospel, with a commission to drive out devils" (3:15). It is thus no accident that exorcism is the first miracle in Mark's Gospel, for the demons know who Jesus is and thereby bear unwitting testimony to his lordship (1:24, 34; 5:7).

The exorcisms may also be intended as clues or foretastes of the new order that God was inaugurating through Jesus. By including accounts of the miraculous, Mark was identifying who belonged to the new covenant community and who did not. Jesus parted company with his own people because by his healings and exorcisms he violated the Jewish laws of purity and separation. His first exorcism was carried out on the Sabbath (1:32-37) in defiance of the rule that set the seventh day apart from the rest of the week and prohibited any unnecessary work being done on it. He touched and healed people who were considered ritually unclean, such as lepers and menstruating women (1:40-45; 5:25-34). He cured a demoniac who was regarded by the Jewish authorities as being beyond the pale because he lived among tombs in pagan territory (5:1-2). He even carried on his healing ministry outside the land of Israel, mingling freely with non-Jews (7:31-37). Jesus' medical skills are hardly ever mentioned because Mark's intention was not to compare him with other healers but to show how, in him, God's purposes were being fulfilled in a new way.[6]

A final reason for Mark's interest in exorcisms is related to the one bald reference he makes to Jesus' struggle with Satan: "Thereupon the Spirit sent him away into the wilderness, and there he remained for forty days tempted by Satan" (1:12). The temptation experience is interpreted as a trial of strength between the Messiah and the devil in which the Messiah won a decisive but not a final victory. From that moment onwards Jesus' ministry is seen as a spiritual war between himself and Satan. The powers of evil challenged him continuously, especially in every form of illness, both physical and mental. But they could not vanquish him because he had already defeated the prince of darkness during his forty days in the wilderness. In Jesus' own words, "No one can break into a strong man's house and make off with his goods unless he has first tied the strong man up: then he can ransack the house" (3:27). If those

6. See, e.g., H. C. Kee, *Medicine, Miracle and Magic in New Testament Times* (Cambridge: Cambridge University Press, 1986), pp. 78f.

scholars are correct who regard the temptation as the initial binding of Satan, then the exorcisms were the "mopping-up operations" of whatever was left of Satan's cohorts. The struggle would continue throughout Jesus' ministry and in the ministry of the Church. Such operations were certain to succeed because Satan himself had been immobilized. As victories over demons they represent Jesus' ultimate victory over evil.

Last Words?

At midday a darkness fell over the whole land, which lasted till three in the afternoon; and at three Jesus cried aloud, "Eli, Eli, lema sabachthani?", which means, "My God, my God, why hast thou forsaken me!" Some of the bystanders, on hearing this, said, "Hark, he is calling Elijah." A man ran and soaked a sponge in sour wine and held it to his lips on the end of a cane. "Let us see," he said, "if Elijah will come to take him down." Then Jesus gave a loud cry and died. And the curtain of the temple was torn in two from top to bottom. And when the centurion who was standing opposite him saw how he died, he said, "Truly this man was a son of God." (mg. or "the Son of God.")

Mark 15:33-39

THE EXPERIENCE OF DEATH both frightens and fascinates us. That is why human beings have always been interested in the last words uttered by those whom they have loved and admired. The dying are further up the line than we are, and perhaps, who knows, they can see something of what is beyond.

For this reason their final words are particularly significant. Exit lines are often a drama of truth telling, of nothing left to hide, nothing more to lose.

This, however, is not always the case. Some last words, while precious to the hearer because they are final, are not necessarily profound. Some are tinged with humour. The widowed Queen Victoria proposed to pay a final visit to Prime Minister Benjamin Disraeli as he lay dying. Informed of this by his physician, Disraeli said, "Why should I see her? She'll only want me to give a message to Albert." King George V had recovered from a serious illness by convalescing on doctor's orders in the English seaside resort of Bognor Regis. Seven years later, when he was on his deathbed, it was suggested to him that he pay a return visit to the town in the hope of a similar result. But the king was too far gone this time. He responded by saying, "Bugger Bognor," and promptly expired. Perhaps some sort of posthumous award for sharp terminal repartee should go to an uncle of Oliver Wendell Holmes. As he lay on his Boston deathbed, a nurse kept feeling his feet and explained to someone in the room, "If his feet are warm he's alive; no one ever died with his feet warm." Holmes awoke from his coma long enough to observe, "John Rogers did." Rogers was a sixteenth-century English Protestant divine who was tried for heresy and burnt at the stake. The most poignant last words must surely be those of the deaf composer Beethoven: "I shall hear in heaven."

While it must be recognized that the classic exit line is by now a dying art, it was very much alive in biblical times. In the Old Testament we find recorded the final utterances of Jacob, Moses, and David, to name but three. In the Book of Acts the final words of the first martyr Stephen are carefully preserved: "Lord, do not hold this sin against them" (7:60). But of course the most famous last words are those of Jesus of

Nazareth. There is, however, no agreement among the evangelists what those words were. Mark, Luke, and John all differ. (Matthew doesn't count because he copies Mark — if, as most scholars believe, we are correct in assuming that Mark was the first Gospel to be written.) Three of "the seven last words" are from Luke, three are from John, and one is from Mark and Matthew. The three in Luke are not repeated in any other Gospel, the three in John are not repeated in any other Gospel, and the one found in Mark is repeated only by Matthew. According to Mark, Jesus' final utterance was, "My God, My God, why hast thou forsaken me?"; according to Luke, "Father, into thy hands I commit my spirit" (23:46); and according to John he said, "It is accomplished!" (19:30). Thus there are three versions of the last words to choose from, and they are all in the Bible.

But because of their very nature, the final utterances of Jesus, like those of anyone else, can only be approximately verified. Are "the seven last words" historical, in the sense that they were actually spoken by Jesus and heard by the bystanders, or are they the creations of the first Christians, put on the lips of Jesus and then incorporated into the narrative with instruction and proclamation in mind? Scholars cannot agree. Those who regard the words recorded by Mark as secondary argue that they were inserted by the early Church in order to explain the "loud cry" of verse 37, which was interpreted as a cry of dereliction and anguish. Those who take them as the authentic words of Jesus insist that no member of the nascent Christian community would have invented such an offensive "last word," which portrays a despairing and doubting Jesus. It seems that the question of historicity must remain open, but there is at least a possibility that the words were spoken by Jesus himself. At the place of execution, the dying were surrounded by relatives, friends, and enemies. There were plenty of attentive witnesses who could hear, and would repeat, what the crucified said. It is therefore by no means impossible that Jesus uttered all that the evangelists report, and presumably very much more. But the authors of the Gospels did not attempt, or intend, to include everything. They simply retained those words that seemed to them to be significant. Here I will concentrate on the Marcan version only, partly because the words that Mark chose to record are so problematic for Christians. How could one who was so close to God experience the absence of God?

People who work as spiritual counselors to the terminally ill speak of the value that familiar hymns possess in times of crisis. Theological truth seems to be more comforting, and seemingly easier to grasp, if it rhymes. There is a lot to be said for hymnbooks, even new ones. The Psalter was, and still is, the hymnbook of the synagogue. According to Mark, it was one of the hymns in this book that was on Jesus' lips when he died. He recited the first verse of Psalm 22. It is noteworthy that of the thirteen Old Testament texts quoted or alluded to in the passion narratives of the Gospels, five come from Psalm 22, two from Psalm 69, and one from Psalm 31. All these psalms were originally prayers for help by a sufferer in time of need. We shall now consider Psalm 22:1 in two ways: first in its original setting, and secondly as the last utterance of Christ.

Original Setting

Psalm 22 divides naturally into two distinct parts: a complaint and a hymn of thanksgiving. The complaint, which comprises the first twenty-one verses, is a prayer for help in which the author laments his situation by describing vividly the trouble he is in and calling on a seemingly unresponsive God to deliver him. The trouble to which he refers is experienced in relation to God, other people, and himself. The absence of God's providential care is noted in spatial and temporal categories — not only is God far away, he is absent day and night (vv. 1-2). In contrast to the distant God, "trouble is near" (v. 11). The enemies of the psalmist surround him; they come close to mock and taunt him.

> All who see me jeer at me,
> make mouths at me and wag their heads. (v. 7)

To convey the seriousness of the situation, the author describes these "others" as dangerous animals ready to attack and maim him.

> A herd of bulls surrounds me,
> great bulls of Bashan beset me.
> Ravening and roaring lions
> open their mouths wide against me.
> The huntsmen are all about me;
> a band of ruffians rings me round,
> and they have hacked off my hands and my feet.
>
> (vv. 12-13, 16)

Finally, he concludes that his life is almost over, since he bears all the physical signs of imminent death and those who watch him are already coveting his wardrobe.

> My strength drains away like water
> and all my bones are loose.
> My heart has turned to wax and melts within me.
> My mouth is dry as a potsherd,
> and my tongue sticks to my jaw;
> I am laid low in the dust of death.

I tell my tale of misery,
while they look on and gloat.
They share out my garments among them
and cast lots for my clothes. (vv. 14-15, 17-18)

But interspersed with this litany of complaints are assertions of trust in God and appeals for help.

But thou art he who drew me from the womb,
who laid me at my mother's breast.
Upon thee was I cast at birth;
from my mother's womb thou hast been my God.
Be not far from me,
for trouble is near, and I have no helper.
(vv. 9-11. See also vv. 19-21)

The second half of the psalm (vv. 22-31) is totally different. Now everything has changed. Instead of prayer for help we have praise for help.

I will declare thy fame to my brethren;
I will praise thee in the midst of the assembly. (v. 22)

Instead of mockers and evildoers, the congregation of the faithful surround the author. Because God has answered him and rescued him, he is at pains to share such glad tidings not only with fellow believers but also with "all the families of the nations" (v. 27). All must be summoned to join in worship with those who recognize the sovereignty of the God of Israel.

But in spite of the obvious division between verse 21 and 22, many commentators regard the psalm as a unity. They see in it a comprehensiveness that transcends the different moods and styles of the two halves. In the interval between the two parts the author's prayer for deliverance has been answered, so that the theme of the psalm is "seeking and finding God." Essentially it is a song of faith and trust.

Like many other psalms, this one also was probably composed for use in worship. Its contents are typical rather than specific. There may have been an actual occasion behind it, but it is more likely that it was written to enable worshippers to express themselves when faced with suffering and need. As such, it would have been used as part of a thanksgiving ceremony when a group gathered to celebrate a friend's deliverance, or by pious Jews to express their faith as they faced illness and death.

The question with which the psalm opens,

> My God, my God why hast thou forsaken me
> and art so far from saving me, from heeding my groans?

is not a quiet, meditative and philosophical question. Rather it is an anguished cry from the heart; it is a protest verging on despair. The psalmist looks God in the eye and expresses rage and bewilderment. He calls God to account. We hear the poignant voice of someone who suffers every kind of misfortune and yet holds fast to the God of Israel. In his lament he questions God's goodness, but also lays claim to him. Though ultimately there is progression in the author's thought from doubt to faith, the tension remains throughout the psalm. The Bible suggests frequently that there is room for protest and doubt in our response to God — witness Psalm 73, and especially the Book of Job — because so many inexplicable things happen. It is a response with which we can all identify at some point or other in our lives.

But despite the immediate impression of protest and despair given by this verse, it is significant that the first four words are "My God, my God." The author is not an unbeliever, as the possessive pronoun *my* indicates. Though desperate, he begins with a confession of faith. Even at the lowest level of dereliction, he is saying his prayers. Despite his anguished question, he recognizes the existence of a personal God who cares for him and hears his voice. The very asking of the question is an act of supreme faith. To presume that God was involved with him at all was a profound spiritual commitment. But paradoxically the survival of his faith against all odds makes his suffering harder, not easier, to bear. If he did not believe in the existence of a loving God who intervenes in human history, he would have no problem. God had been real to him in the past, a help in times of trouble. Now, in the hour of his greatest need, he feels abandoned. When he needs it most, the divine consolation is lacking. He is dismayed at the silence and distance of God because he expected a response, however faint, to his cry for help. In his own eyes he has a right to expect divine intervention, for had not the Lord of history made a covenant with his chosen people? Surely he could expect more from God than from an idol. The author's faith in the God of the fathers compounds his suffering.

The experience of God as an elusive presence is not confined to the Bible. A twentieth-century African famine can be a major obstacle to faith for someone who believes in an all-good and all-powerful God, rather than in blind fate. For over two thousand years Jews have asked the same question as the psalmist when confronted with hostility and persecution. Holocaust survivors recall how fellow Jews asked aloud if God had forsaken them, using these familiar opening words of Psalm 22. As they faced certain death from the Nazis, they were puzzled at God's inability or unwillingness to intervene, and they remonstrated with him as the prophet Isaiah had done centuries before:

Why didst thou not rend the heavens and come down?
. . . then would thy name be know to thy enemies
and nations tremble at thy coming. (64:1-2)

Why did the merciful and omnipotent savior, who brought his
people out of Egypt, not liberate the camps?

However, taken *as a whole,* Psalm 22 is anything but a cry
of despair. Protest, yes, but not hopelessness. During the second
half it soars to the heights of praise and thanksgiving in response to God answering a plea for help.

I will declare thy fame to my brethren;
    I will praise thee in the midst of the assembly. . . .
For he has not scorned the downtrodden,
        nor shrunk in loathing from his plight,
        nor hidden his face from him,
        but gave heed to him when he cried out.
Thou dost inspire my praise in the full assembly;
        and I will pay my vows before all who fear thee. . . .
This shall be told of the Lord to future generations;
        and they shall justify him,
        declaring to a people yet unborn
        that this was his doing. (vv. 22-31)

The psalm was written by one who was indeed once in
the depths of despair, but whose faith in God's saving power
had in the end been vindicated. In the presence of the congregation he acknowledged divine help by bearing personal testimony to it. So Psalm 22 is classed not as a psalm of lament
but as one of confidence and trust, a song that celebrates
ultimate victory. It is regarded as a cry of faith, not of despair.
We do not have to read the whole psalm to hear that cry of
faith, it is present even in the opening verse. The very recog-

nition by the psalmist of a sense of abandonment is itself an act of faith.

From the Cross

Assuming that Luke and John knew the Marcan Passion, why didn't they accept the last words as reported in it? Why, according to them, doesn't Jesus die protesting and alone? Why do they soften the last moments of his earthly life? For this is what they have done. In Luke the last words of Jesus were words of trust and confidence. Quoting again from the Psalter, Jesus commends himself to God: "Into thy hands, O Lord, I commend my spirit" (Ps. 31:5). In John his last words are words of victory, words of accomplishment; he had done, he had "finished" or "accomplished," what he came to do. In neither of them is there any hint of dereliction. Why not? We can but guess. Could it be that Luke and John were embarrassed by the last words as recorded in Mark? They may have found them mysterious and liable to misinterpretation. Perhaps they did not want to believe that the Lord of Life had died an abandoned derelict. What image, they may have asked, would this provide for his followers?

Given the reaction of Luke and John, it is not surprising that attempts have been made to defend Mark's version of the last words and to allow them to stand as they are. There are two common explanations. The first rests on the interpretation that Psalm 22 is anything but a cry of despair. It may start that way, but it ends with complete confidence in God's protection and mercy. It has been suggested that what Jesus intended to express was the faith and hope of the psalmist, not his disillusionment. Though he quoted only the first verse, those who heard him would have recognized a psalm of trust, for such

147

quotations recall not just the text but the whole context. Citing the opening words of any portion of Scripture was, in Jewish tradition, a way of referring to the entire passage. Therefore, because more than the first words may be implied here, it is possible to argue that the early Church could have supposed that the whole psalm was intended in this context. This interpretation is linked to the view that the final "loud cry" from the cross was not one of dereliction but of faith in ultimate vindication by God. It is suggested that Mark's choice of last words is not meant to be a description by Jesus of his own despair, but only the first line of Psalm 22 quoted with reference to what follows. Jesus took on his lips "the inspired utterance of Jewish piety," and made the psalmist's expression of faith his own. In other words, the more obvious meaning is softened.

The second explanation takes the words at face value and sees in them a spontaneous cry of desolation on the part of Jesus. This would seem to be more in line with Mark's general ethos and purpose, for there is no hint in the Gospel itself that the author intended his readers to think of the whole psalm. Furthermore, there is no evidence that Jesus used Scripture in this way. If he did, would he not have done so more often? If we believe that the whole psalm was included in this one quotation, we may well miss the point that Mark is trying to make, for throughout his Gospel he deliberately presents us with a picture of a suffering and lonely Jesus. Suffering was the inevitable consequence of preaching the good news of God because such action brought Jesus into conflict with Satan and the religious authorities. Though this suffering must surely include the pain of scourging and crucifixion, Mark, like the other evangelists, does not dwell on the physical aspect. This reticence has been explained as Mark's desire to show that the suffering of Jesus goes far beyond the agony experienced by the crucified. If the evangelist is to impress upon his readers the enormity of Jesus' suffering, he must show that it involves more than the physical pain endured by thousands of others during the Roman occupation of Palestine. Certainly, crucifixion was barbaric and cruel, but it was not the most brutal form of execution possible. Furthermore, a six-hour ordeal, which is what Jesus underwent, was not sufficiently unusual to make a lasting impression on readers in the ancient world. If he had lingered on the cross for several days, as very many did, a detailed description of his death might have been considered worthwhile. But Jesus was dead long before sundown.

Despite his reluctance to portray the crucifixion in any detail, Mark's central theme throughout his Gospel is the suffering Messiah. But instead of giving a detailed account of the physical agony endured by Jesus, he concentrates on his rejection and isolation. It is the loneliness of Jesus that Mark emphasizes in the crucifixion. This alienation is prominent from the very beginning of the Gospel. During his Galilean ministry, Jesus was condemned by the religious authorities; misunderstood by his family; rejected by his neighbors; betrayed, denied, and abandoned by his disciples. When he was brought to Golgotha he was utterly alone. For Mark, this abandonment and alienation is the ultimate form of suffering. But Jesus is abandoned not only by friends and family but also by God. The cry of dereliction that he attributes to Jesus therefore rings true. It should not be softened or explained away, and it is worth noting that in this Mark is followed by Matthew.

To be forsaken is to be cut off from what gives meaning to life, what holds us together, what enables us to keep going. If we have experienced this, it will give us a tiny clue as to what was happening in Jerusalem on that Friday afternoon. Jesus defined himself by his closeness to God. He spoke of God as his Father. During his ministry he had gone into desert places to be alone with him. There was a union between them: "I and the Father are one." This total identity is described in the creeds as "being of one substance" with the Father. This closeness had given him the strength and courage to take whatever the world threw at him. But suddenly God withdrew. Nothing now sustained him. This is the only time in the New Testament that Jesus calls God "God" and not "Abba," Father. He plumbed the very depths of human experience. This is what Mark wants us to remember.

The Marcan Passion began with an act of recognition (14:2-9) when Jesus was recognized as the Messiah by an unknown woman — in the eyes of the religious establishment, a second-class citizen. It ends with another act of recognition, this time by a Gentile — in the eyes of the authorities, an unbeliever. When the Roman centurion heard the last words and witnessed the final scene on Calvary, he said, "Truly this man was the Son of God." Both acts of recognition would be vindicated three days later.

A Hard Saying

Turning to the Jews who had believed him, Jesus said . . . "Your father is the devil and you choose to carry out your father's desires. He was a murderer from the beginning, and is not rooted in the truth; there is no truth in him. When he tells a lie he is speaking his own language, for he is a liar and the father of lies. But I speak the truth and therefore you do not believe me. Which of you can prove me in the wrong? If what I say is true, why do you not believe me? He who has God for his father listens to the words of God. You are not God's children; that is why you do not listen."

John 8:31, 44-47

SINCE THE END OF THE SECOND WORLD WAR, many detailed accounts have been written of anti-Jewish polemic in Christian literature. With very few exceptions, they begin with the major theologians of the second century AD. In almost every case, the opening chapter contains a detailed account of the so-called *adversus Judaeos* writings of such prominent ecclesiastics as Justin Martyr, Melito of Sardis, and Ignatius of Antioch.

151

Spurred into action by the claim that there is a direct link between the Nazi Holocaust and the Church's negative attitude towards Judaism, scholars have subjected the views and recommendations of the early Christian Fathers about the Jews to close scrutiny. Their painstaking research has shown that the virulent hatred felt by Christians towards the Jewish people is never far from the surface in the works of many influential teachers and preachers from the second century onwards. As a result, leading ecclestiastical historians insist that the anti-Judaism of some of the Church's greatest theologians contains the seeds of modern antisemitism.

Although Christians are ready to scour patristic texts for the slightest hint of what has been described as "the teaching of contempt," many of them are reluctant to subject the foundation documents of the faith to the same critique. What may be true of the second century is not, in their view, true of the first. While the works of the Fathers may justly be regarded as the source of much of the persecution endured by Jews at Gentile hands over the centuries, such a charge cannot be leveled at the New Testament. Many biblical scholars are adamant that there is no connection between the markedly prejudicial and damaging statements about Jews and Judaism found in Christian Scripture and the barbaric antisemitism of Hitler. They refuse to believe that what has been termed the "theological antisemitism" of the Christian era has any basis in the New Testament. They insist, for instance, that the hard sayings about the Pharisees attributed to Jesus and the pointed remarks of Paul about the inferiority of Judaism should in no way be regarded as having augmented the sufferings of the Jews over the past two thousand years. They do not accept that such phrases as "His blood be upon us and upon our children," which, according to Matthew 27:26, was on the lips of the crowd of onlookers at Calvary, may have contributed to the ongoing persecution of the Jewish people. They do not concede that one of the most belligerent references to Jews in all Christian Scripture, found in 1 Thessalonians 2:16 where the author states that they are the deserved recipients of God's wrath, may have been taken by countless generations of Christians as license to harass and even murder their Jewish neighbors.

However, an increasing number of commentators are coming to the conclusion that the New Testament does have a part to play in the shameful treatment meted out to Jews by Christians for almost twenty centuries. They insist that the image of the Jew portrayed by the biblical authors has contributed substantially to the persecution suffered by the Jewish people. As one would expect, certain texts have been singled out for close scrutiny. But before turning to a specific verse, a survey of current scholarship in this area is in order.

The Taproot of Anti-Semitism

The view expressed by the Roman Catholic scholar Bruce Vawter in 1968 is typical of a number of Christian theologians who deny any possible link between Nazi antisemitism and the New Testament. In his view, to suggest that there is "a straight ideological line linking the Gospels with the furnaces of Auschwitz . . . is obvious nonsense. Gruesome as are the annals of antisemitism, Christian and other, it is doubtful that the Gospels have had very much of a real part to play in any of them."[1] While he recognizes the existence of hostility towards Jews in Scripture, Vawter believes that it is subsequent generations of Christians who must take the blame for fostering the

---

1. Bruce Vawter, "Are the Gospels Anti-Semitic?" *Journal of Ecumenical Studies* 5 (1968): p. 487.

antisemitism of later times because they quoted the Bible in support of anti-Jewish actions. The seeds of persecution were not sown by the writers of the New Testament. Another Roman Catholic, J. B. Sheerin, in evaluating the past in Catholic-Jewish relations at a conference of Jewish and Christian theologians, could claim categorically that "the sacred books do not condemn the Jewish people."[2]

Increasingly, scholars have taken issue with statements such as these. Jewish theologians in particular have been vocal in their disagreement. Eliezer Berkovitz, who has written extensively on the Holocaust, claims that "Christianity's New Testament has been the most dangerous antisemitic tract in history. Its hatred-charged diatribes against the Pharisees and the Jews have poisoned the hearts and minds of millions and millions of Christians for almost two millennia. Without it Hitler's *Mein Kampf* could never have been written."[3] Strong words, which are totally unacceptable to many Christians. But Berkovitz, an Orthodox Jew, is supported by Samuel Sandmel, a teacher at the Cincinnati college that trains rabbis for the Reform branch of Judaism. Sandmel was a meticulous scholar who devoted much of his career to promoting dialogue and understanding between Christians and Jews. In the last book that he wrote, *Anti-Semitism in the New Testament?*, he concludes that the Christian Scriptures do contain antisemitic elements. After examining the evidence book by book he feels bound to say, "It is simply not correct to exempt the New Testament from anti-Semitism and to allocate it to later periods of history. It must be said that innumerable Christians have indeed purged themselves of anti-Semitism, but its expression is to be found in Christian Scripture for all to read." While applauding Chris-

---

2. P. Scharper, ed., *Torah and Gospel* (New York: Orbis, 1966), p. 25.
3. Eliezer Berkovitz, "Facing the Truth," *Judaism* 27 (1978): p. 325.

tians for rising above antisemitism, he states unreservedly that "the presence of anti-Semitism in the New Testament is what presents the occasion for rising above it."[4]

Jewish scholars are not the only ones to come to this conclusion; their view is shared by reputable Christian scholars. The most extensive investigation to date of the negation of Judaism in the Bible is that carried out by N. A. Beck, a professor at Texas Lutheran College. The subtitle of his book *Mature Christianity* indicates the author's concern: "The recognition and repudiation of the anti-Jewish polemic of the New Testament." In her controversial study of the theological roots of antisemitism, *Faith and Fratricide*, the Roman Catholic theologian Rosemary Ruether argues that parts of the New Testament were *intended* by their authors to turn Christians against Jews. She asks pointedly, "Is it possible to say 'Jesus is the Messiah' without, implicitly or explicitly, saying at the same time 'and the Jews be damned'?"[5] James Parkes, the Anglican cleric who ranks as a doyen in the field of Christian-Jewish relations, writing some fifty years after he commenced his study of the subject, states categorically that "it is dishonest henceforth to refuse to face the fact that the basic root of modern antisemitism lies squarely in the Gospels and the rest of the New Testament."[6]

Any consideration of the vexed question concerning the biblical roots of antisemitism must, therefore, take account of two diametrically opposed views. Both are espoused by distin-

---

4. Samuel Sandmel, *Anti-Semitism in the New Testament?* (Philadelphia: Fortress Press, 1978), pp. 144, 162.

5. Rosemary Ruether, *Faith and Fratricide* (New York: Seabury Press, 1974), p. 246.

6. Preface to A. T. Davies, ed., *Antisemitism and the Foundations of Christianity* (New York: Paulist Press, 1979), p. xi. For the most recent treatment of this issue see L. C. Freudmann, *Antisemitism in the New Testament* (London and Lanham, Maryland: University Press of America, 1994).

guished scholars who are acutely conscious of the persecution suffered by the Jewish people and are determined to eradicate the possibility of another Holocaust. However, the lack of agreement between the two sides suggests that the issue will remain on the theological agenda for some time to come and will continue to be vigorously debated. Both views are based on differing concepts of the nature and purpose of Holy Scripture.

The first view, that which denies any connection between the New Testament and later pogroms, is governed primarily by dogmatic considerations. Its protagonists engage in an ideological defense of the New Testament in order to ward off the criticism that parts of it are contaminated by anti-Jewish prejudice. In their opinion, to claim that Christian Scripture is "sacred" is tantamount to saying that it is morally unassailable, free from every blemish, and immune to human fallibility. It is the inspired and inerrant "Word of God," whose absolute authority is upheld by the oft-quoted formula "the Bible says." While the early Church Fathers may be justly condemned for their rabid anti-Judaism because their writings are not considered to be inspired, the same criticism cannot be leveled at the New Testament. A double standard comes into operation simply because, in dealing with the Bible, the inquirer stands on holy ground.

Proponents of the second view, those Jews and Christians who see a connection between Auschwitz and the Gospels, are not as reluctant to submit the Bible to searching criticism. They recognize that although Scripture is sacred, it is linked to time and space; it reflects historical circumstances. And inasmuch as it was written and preserved by fallible people, it can never be free from a human element. Since the New Testament reflects the difficulties and tensions felt by the nascent Church during the first Christian century, the circumstances surrounding its origin should be considered by all who seek to interpret its message in the contemporary world. The implications inherent in the fact that the Word of God comes to us in the words of men must be faced. Whatever the intention of the biblical authors, some New Testament texts are, to say the least, exceedingly unflattering to Jews. Because of their hostile nature, they have been used to provide antisemitism, both theological and secular, with a degree of legitimation. A literal reading of anti-Jewish passages in the Bible has provided those who wish to persecute Jews with ample justification for doing so.

The debate between these two standpoints is essentially concerned with authority. The central question is, Have we the right to criticize our own religious traditions? May we legitimately stand in judgment on Scripture? Are we justified in repudiating certain New Testament passages because they are damaging to Jews? Those who use such terms as "inerrant" and "infallible" in relation to the Bible will deny the existence of such a right. In the past, however, our Christian forefathers had no qualms about engaging in subjective interpretation of their own Scriptures, namely the Old Testament. The early Church happily pressed selected portions of the Hebrew Bible into service to prove the superiority of Christianity, while neglecting the rest. Appropriate passages were used as a quarry for messianic prophecies and listed as "proof texts" to demonstrate that the Messiah had come in Jesus of Nazareth. But the laws governing diet and circumcision, to take but two examples, were either ignored or given a meaning other than the literal. Much of the Old Testament was spiritualized or allegorized by Christian commentators in order to accommodate it to the Church's teaching.

But such selectivity and reinterpretation was not confined to the Hebrew Bible; it was applied to the New Testament as well. The stipulations about nonretaliation (Matt. 5:39), almsgiving (Matt. 5:42), self-denial (Matt. 16:24), celibacy

(1 Cor. 7), and the role of women in the Church (1 Tim. 2:12) have been either ignored in practice or spiritualized by most Christians. Martin Luther felt justified in dismissing the Letter of James and calling into question its place in the canon of Scripture. He referred to it as an "epistle of straw" because James, by insisting that faith without works was dead, contradicted the Pauline concept of salvation by unmerited grace, which Luther regarded as the essence of the Christian gospel. If some aspects of New Testament teaching can justifiably be repudiated, in the sense of their being regarded as not valid or binding for contemporary Christians, cannot the same principle be applied to passages that have proved injurious for almost two millennia to persons outside the Christian community?

Bearing in mind the difference of opinion expressed by scholars about the existence of anti-Jewish polemic in Christianity's foundation documents, and recognizing that, for both sides, the issue is far from settled, we shall turn to a specific verse. Attention will now be focused on a New Testament text that contains a particularly "hard saying" for those who are ecumenically minded and are conscious of the appalling record of the Christian Church in its relationship with Jews for over nineteen hundred years. In John 8:44 Jesus says to the Jews who had believed in him: "Your father is the devil and you choose to carry out your father's desires." The claim that the Jews are the offspring and agents of Satan is regarded as one of the main factors contributing to their humiliation and debasement at the hands of Christians. An attempt will now be made to show how this verse from John not only had an adverse influence on Christian thought for centuries but also, albeit unintentionally, contributed to the vicious antisemitism of the twentieth century, beginning with a brief account of the systematic attempt by the Christian Church to demonize the Jews.

Children of Satan

In 1936 the Nazis published a picture book for children that contained an artist's impression of a Jew. The caption under the picture of a pot-bellied individual with bulging eyes, a hooked nose, and thick lips, reads: "The father of the Jews is the devil." Though such a notion played a prominent part in Hitler's antisemitic propaganda, it was not original to twentieth-century Germany. It had been voiced four hundred years previously by Martin Luther. In his infamous tract *On the Jews and their Lies,* written three years before his death in 1546, he concluded that since the Jews were no longer God's people, in that they had been replaced by the Church, they must be "the devil's people." As the objects of God's wrath, they had been handed over to Lucifer. Their spiritual blindness, which led them to reject Christ, was induced by Satan because the whole nation had been "possessed by the devil and his angels." He told his readers that whenever they saw a genuine Jew, they could with a good conscience cross themselves and say, "There goes a devil incarnate."

Luther does more than theorize; he makes practical suggestions about the appropriate action with regard to Satan's brood. He warns his fellow Christians of the dangers inherent in even associating with them and makes seven specific recommendations to the German princes on how to deal with them: their synagogues should be burned; their homes destroyed; their prayer books confiscated; their rabbis forbidden to teach; their right to safe conduct on the highways denied; their valuables appropriated; their young taken into forced labor. He concludes: "To sum up, dear princes and nobles who have Jews in your domains, if this advice of mine does not suit you, then find a better one, so that you and we may all be free of this insufferable devilish burden — the Jews." A penetrating and pitiless passage that has been described by one historian as "the bitterest anti-Jewish tirade in all Christian literature."[7] Here I am not concerned to excuse or explain Luther's views, but simply to draw attention to the antisemitic potential inherent in his recommendations, all of which stem from his demonization of the Jews.

But if the Nazis cannot be credited with originality in linking the Jews with the devil, neither can Luther. For in his anti-Jewish tirades the great architect of the Protestant Reformation was simply stepping into the past and regurgitating the slanders of preceding centuries. In the late Middle Ages interest in the devil as a malevolent being who could assume human form swept through Europe. In wood, stone, and parchment Satan was presented as a frightening figure, presumably in the hope of terrifying all who saw such representations into good behavior. He was frequently associated with animals, especially dogs, monkeys, snakes, and pigs. But his favorite was the goat, whose characteristics he often shares in that he has horns, a beard, a tail, and cloven hooves. When he is depicted as a human, he appears deformed and ugly, with distorted facial features. His limbs are twisted and his hair dishevelled. He has bulging eyes with no eyebrows, a prominent nose, and a protruding lower lip. If he were invisible, his presence could always be detected by his pungent, sulphurous smell; the opposite, presumably, of "the odor of sanctity" — whatever that is. Next to black, his favorite color is red or ginger; he dresses in red and has red hair and a red beard.

All these satanic features — animal characteristics, physical ugliness, a fondness for the color red, and a pungent stench — are employed by medieval craftsmen and writers to depict

7. J. Marcus, *The Jew in the Mediaeval World* (New York: Schocken, 1960), p. 165.

Jews as the ally of Lucifer in a deliberate attempt to demonize them. In the art of the Middle Ages Jews appear with ugly, demonic faces. Their bodies are hideous and misshapen. They are skillful at hiding their horns with the pointed hats they are required to wear as a distinguishing mark. Their hair is often red, and they are identified by a reddish-yellow piece of cloth sown onto the outer garment, the infamous "Jewish badge" decreed by the Fourth Lateran Council in 1215. In depictions of scenes from the gospels, Judas Iscariot is easily recognizable because of his red hair. Like Satan, Jews are often portrayed as apes, which was also an ancient symbol of the Synagogue. Their lechery linked them to the goat. But perhaps the most invidious association was that made between Jews and pigs. Not only were pigs associated with evil and Satan, they were also characterized by filth and stench. An unclean animal was an ideal symbol for an unclean people, who, like the devil, could always be recognized by their offensive odor — the stench of moral corruption. Popular preachers and the authors of miracle and passion plays made certain that the satanic nature of Jews was fully appreciated by the common people. In sermons and plays they invariably describe Jews as "devils from hell, enemies of the human race." When Jews died at the stake, devils would rush onto the stage to carry off their souls.

The caricature created by these artists and writers has had a long life, surviving into the twentieth century. Shakespeare reflects the common perception in Elizabethan England when he writes in *The Merchant of Venice,* "Certainly the Jew is the very devil incarnal." Though redheads are to be found aplenty in Celtic countries, the notion that red hair is a specifically Jewish trait is not uncommon. It is found, for instance, in the works of Charles Dickens. In *Sketches by Boz* he writes, "Holywell Street we despise; the red-headed and red-whiskered Jews who forcibly haul you into their squalid houses, and thrust you into a suit of clothes, whether you will or not, we detest." He includes the same characteristic in his portrayal of Fagin in *Oliver Twist:* "Standing over them, with a toasting-fork in his hand, was a very old, shrivelled Jew, whose villainous-looking and repulsive face was obscured by a quantity of matted red hair."

While the efforts of medieval popularizers to demonize the Jews met with considerable success, credit for originality cannot go to them either. They simply echo the teachings handed down to them by their predecessors, for the concept of the Jew as the child of Satan long antedates the Middle Ages; it is prominent in the works of the early Church Fathers. While the pictorial form of anti-Judaism was not a feature of early Christianity, contempt for Jews was a marked feature of the voluminous literature produced by a small but elite band of theologians. When the Fathers were confronted by heresy and disbelief, they relied not on art and sculpture to crush and ridicule their rivals, but on the persuasive power of the spoken and written word. They wrote tracts against everybody and everything, and when these failed in their objective, as they invariably did, they rebuked, fined, exiled, and excommunicated their opponents.

Because the Jews were perceived to be a threat to the Church, every theologian of note deemed it necessary to write at least one tract against them. In the published sermons of Eusebius of Alexandria the devil refers casually and frequently to his "old friends, the Jews." Gregory of Nyssa calls the Jews "the advocates of the devil." John Chrysostom, one of the leading lights of the Orthodox Church and later Bishop of Constantinople, preached a series of eight sermons in 386, when he was a parish priest in Antioch, "against Judaizing Christians." In them he made a determined effort to dissuade members of his congregation from fraternizing with Jews, by claiming that "the synagogues of the Jews are the homes of idolatry and devils." He states that it is his intention "to show that demons dwell in the synagogue, not only in the place itself, but also in the very souls of the Jews." He concludes that "if the Jews are acting against God, must they not be serving the demons?"

This virulent hatred of Jews was based, in part, on a specifically Christian interpretation of Old Testament texts. In their reading of the Jewish Scriptures, the Fathers regarded every curse as being applicable to Jews but every blessing to Christians. Any negative feature prefigured Judaism; any positive feature prefigured Christianity. For example, when Rebecca asked God to explain why the twins she was expecting were so restless, the answer, according to the author of Genesis, was "Two nations in your womb, two peoples, going their own ways from birth! One shall be stronger than the other; the older shall be servant to the younger" (Gen. 25:23). The Fathers regarded this reference to Jacob and Esau as a prophecy of the tension between Christianity and Judaism. The stronger and the younger was the Christian, the weaker and the older was the Jew. Interpreted thus, the verse confirmed the belief that Christianity had displaced Judaism. The Old Testament proved time and again the superiority of the Church over the Synagogue and justified every effort to eradicate Judaism, whether by persecution or by conversion. But with reference to the demonization of the Jews, the primary authority was the New Testament, and in particular John 8:44, which goes far beyond anything Jesus says to his opponents in the Synoptic Gospels.

One obvious difference between the Fourth Gospel and the other three is the way in which the author refers to the enemies of Jesus. While the others identify those who take issue with Jesus' teachings as Pharisees, Sadducees, Scribes, Herodians, or simply "the crowd," John disregards all differences and replaces the restricted wording of his sources with the umbrella term "the Jews." He obliterates the historical distinctions of the earlier records by altering the specific designation of Jesus' opponents and using a general designation. Whereas the Synoptics (Matthew, Mark, and Luke) refer to "the Jews" fifteen times between them, John uses the term seventy times in twenty-one chapters. In almost half of the Johannine instances the reference is derogatory, indicating deep-seated animosity between Jesus and his contemporaries. The Jews persecute Jesus (5:16), speak disapprovingly of him (6:41), and finally seek to kill him (7:1). They are his sworn enemies because they are blind to his teaching (7:35) and sinful in their unbelief (8:24), but above all, because they are the spawn of the devil (8:44). The contrasts to which John was so partial also enabled him to express his dislike of the Jews. Whereas Judaism represented the old way, Jesus introduced "a new commandment," that of love (13:34). The Jews were carnal, but Jesus was spiritual (3:5-6). The Jews were in darkness, whereas Jesus was of the light (1:4). Jewish teachers were hirelings and robbers, while Jesus was "the good shepherd" (10:14). In each of these cases the hostile use of the unqualified term "the Jews" is obvious, not only because of the verbs or phrases attached to it, but because of its larger context. The potential of such references to legitimize anti-Jewish behavior is equally obvious, for the power of such language and thought to shape a hostile attitude towards Jews is very real. Whatever John's intentions were in vilifying the Jews, the antisemitic potential of an uncritical acceptance of every negative statement he makes is only too real.

Neutralizing the Antisemitic Potential

This negative portrayal of the Jews is one reason why some commentators consider the Fourth Gospel to be a most unsuitable text for Jewish-Christian dialogue. E. J. Epp regards it as a "baleful" Gospel, more responsible "than any other book in the canonical body of Christian writings . . . for the frequent anti-Semitic expressions by Christians during the past eighteen or nineteen centuries."[8] "The beloved disciple," as John is often referred to, has also been labeled "the father of anti-Semitism."[9] But equally there are those who claim that John is not as hostile to the Jewish people as is commonly supposed, and have sought to exculpate him from the charge of antisemitism by calling for a clearer understanding of his terminology. They maintain, for example, that the term "the Jews" should not be taken as referring to the whole nation, and have suggested several meanings for it. It could refer simply to the people of Judea (7:1), that is, to the inhabitants of the southern part of Palestine as opposed to those of Galilee in the north. (The Greek form of "the Jews," *hoi Ioudaioi,* makes the possible connection with Judea, *Ioudaia,* easier to understand. A similar use of the part for the whole may be found in the European understanding of "Yankees" to refer to Americans in general, but within the United States the term denotes the inhabitants of a specific geographical area.) It could indicate the religious authorities in Jerusalem (7:13), in the same way as the terms "the French" or "the Germans" may refer to those in France and Germany who make political decisions rather than the population as a whole. It could be used to distinguish one group of the inhab-

8. E. J. Epp, "Anti-Semitism and the Popularity of the Fourth Gospel in Christianity," *Central Conference of American Rabbis Journal* 22 (1975): p. 49.

9. A. T. Davies, *Anti-Semitism and the Christian Mind: The Crisis of Conscience after Auschwitz* (New York: Herder & Herder, 1969), p. 60.

itants of Palestine from another (4:9), such as the distinction between Jews and Samaritans, or to describe customs unfamiliar to Gentiles (7:2). It could be a code word for all, Jews and Gentiles, who did not believe in Jesus (8:22-25). Such explanations, if accepted, put the negative references to "the Jews" into perspective and defuse the situation appreciably.

In the interests of negating the antisemitic potential of the text, another approach may be considered, namely that which seeks to place the Gospel in its correct historical and sociological context. A reconstruction of the Fourth Gospel's milieu at about AD 90 has led scholars to posit the existence of two distinct communities: Jews and Christians. The Jewish community was trying to preserve its identity in the face of Christian evangelism and experiencing a growing number of converts who accepted Jesus as the Messiah but wanted to remain within Judaism. Jewish Christians believed in the divinity of Jesus — an article of faith their opponents could never accept. Eventually these secret believers were expelled from the synagogues and suffered at the hands of the Romans, to whom they had been denounced by the local Jewish leaders. (See John 9:22; 12:42; 16:2-3.) Such violence left "deep scars on the Johannine psyche," and the evangelist reacted by launching a vicious attack on the local Jewish community. His anti-Jewish polemic seems linked to his insistence that Jesus was divine. However, despite such hostility, it must be recognized that John was criticizing those from among *his own people* who had rejected Jesus. Thus the quarrel is essentially an intra-Jewish one, and for this reason many commentators find the term "antisemitism," which was coined in Germany at the end of the last century and implies racial prejudice, to be quite unsuitable to describe John's attitude to his fellow Jews.

The importance of the historical context in which the Gospel was written for our understanding of John's portrayal of the Jews is threefold. First, it mitigates, to a certain extent, his harshness towards them. When we appreciate that his attitude is influenced by the dire circumstances of his own day, namely the crisis experienced by a group of Christians, not only are we are less ready to judge him harshly, we are also less likely to take his words literally. We are ready to excuse such vituperation, for it may be argued that vilifying the other is a part of defining the self. The function of scurrilous and abusive language against Jews, whether it be in the Gospel of John or anywhere else, was to strengthen and encourage Christians struggling to survive and seeking to establish a legitimate identity over against a powerful Jewish community. But for centuries Christian preachers and popularizers paid no attention to the context; they simply took John at his word and interpreted his anti-Judaism literally.

Second, consideration of the historical context reminds us that John expresses timebound prejudices against the Jews of his own age and locality, not global anti-Judaism. Since he was reacting to a specific situation, his words must not be taken out of context and applied to every Jew at all times and in all places. This point has been consistently, and perhaps deliberately, overlooked in the Christian tradition. In his tract *Against the Jews,* written at the beginning of the fifth century, Augustine, the saintly bishop of Hippo in North Africa, was presumably accusing the Jews of his own day of involvment in the Crucifixion when he said to them, "You, in your parents, killed Christ."

Third, it demonstrates that the views of Judaism put forward in the Gospel of John are not representative of Jesus and do not reflect his attitude to the Jews of his day. This helps the reader to appreciate that the Gospel does not necessarily contain the exact words of Jesus, but the meditations of a devoted disciple on the Jesus tradition, and the application of that tradition to a particular Christian community.

If Christian preachers and teachers over the past two millennia had taken such considerations into account with reference to the charge of demonization, the fate of the Jews might have been very different. If they had wrestled, as we now must, with the limitations imposed upon the Bible by the circumstances in which it was written, the Christian perception of the Jew would have been far less negative, and the antisemitic potential of John's Gospel would, to a certain extent, have been neutralized.

Things We Ought to Forget

If anyone thinks to base his claim on externals, I could make a stronger case for myself: circumcised on my eighth day, Israelite by race, of the tribe of Benjamin, a Hebrew born and bred; in my attitude to the law, a Pharisee; in pious zeal, a persecutor of the church; in legal rectitude, faultless. But all such assets I have written off because of Christ. I would say more: I count everything sheer loss, because all is far outweighed by the gain of knowing Christ Jesus my Lord, for whose sake I did in fact lose everything. I count it so much garbage, for the sake of gaining Christ and finding myself incorporate in him, with no righteousness of my own, no legal rectitude, but the righteousness which comes from faith in Christ, given by God in response to faith. All I care for is to know Christ, to experience the power of his resurrection, and to share his sufferings, in growing conformity with his death, if only I may finally arrive at the resurrection from the dead.

It is not to be thought that I have already achieved all this. I have not yet reached perfection, but I press on, hoping to take hold of that for which Christ once took hold of me. My friends, I do not reckon myself to have got hold of it yet. All I

169

can say is this: forgetting what is behind me, and reaching out for that which lies ahead, I press towards the goal to win the prize which is God's call to the life above, in Christ Jesus.

Philippians 3:3-14

ATALANTA, LIKE MOST PRINCESSES in Greek mythology, was a woman of great beauty. But although she was wooed by many eligible suitors, she clearly had a mind of her own. Determined to preserve her independence, she announced that she would marry only the one who beat her in a footrace. She added as an afterthought that if he lost, her competitor must pay for his defeat with his life. In spite of such barbarous terms, a few confident youths attempted to outrun her. But since Atalanta could cover a hundred yards in an amazingly few seconds, it was not long before their severed heads began to appear in the stadium to deter the dilettante. Undaunted by these frightful trophies, Milanion expressed his intention of competing with Atalanta. But before doing so he had the foresight to consult the goddess Venus, who gave him three golden apples with which to further his cause. As Atalanta raced past him, Milanion threw down an apple. The princess stopped to pick it up. This happened three times, with the result that Milanion won. But in the excitement of his nuptials, he forgot to thank Venus, who promptly turned him and his bride into lions. And since there is no evidence to the contrary, presumably they both lived happily ever after.

In his letter to the Philippians, Paul compares the Christian life to a race. Not a race in which there is only one winner, but a race in which every entrant obtains a prize. There is, however, one condition: the race can be won only if the runners disregard what lies behind them. So the apostle couples encouragement to seek the goal with the recommendation to forget the past.

170

He counsels the Christians at Philippi to imitate him, forgetting what is behind, "and reaching out for that which lies ahead" (v. 14). Such advice is not as unrealistic as it may at first appear. Paul does not expect his readers not to remember the past; that would be impossible, for who can choose what they remember or forget? Forgetting in the biblical sense is not what we do when we fail to remember the date of the First Crusade. Rather, it is a deliberate abandonment, a deliberate setting aside of the past, or of certain aspects of the past, in the interests of the present. Those whose Greek is what it used to be will recall that in Greek the present participle (in this case "forgetting") points to an action that is simultaneous with the main verb. The forgetting is continuous, ceaseless, and deliberate; Paul forgets as he runs.

In the good sense "forgetting" denotes the ejection act of the soul, a throwing out of the unworthy and the undesirable. It is the blue pencil of wisdom excising all unnecessary words from the book of life. In the bad sense it describes Israel's willful rejection of the Lord in favor of Baal — witness Jeremiah's condemnation of the false prophets:

> I have heard what the prophets say, the prophets who speak lies in my name and cry, "I have had a dream, a dream!" How long will it be till they change their tune, these prophets who prophesy lies and give voice to their own inventions? By these dreams which they tell one another these men think they will make my people forget my name as their fathers forgot my name for the name of Baal. (23:25-27)

These prophets could never persuade Israel not to remember the Lord, but they tried very hard to make it reject him.

The past to which Paul refers is not entirely clear. He could mean his former life in Judaism, with all the advantages and achievements enumerated earlier in the chapter. In verses 3 and 4 he sets out his credentials and argues that they are impeccable. Not only is he a member of God's chosen people, he is a pious and punctilious Jew. As such, he can make a stronger case than anyone if the criteria for being God's people are national privilege and personal accomplishments. It is more likely, however, that he is referring to his life since his conversion. He is not saying that remembering is not important, far from it; he is too thoroughly steeped in Judaism to think that. He is conscious also of the emerging Christian tradition, which must at all costs be preserved and handed on. But he realizes that memory sometimes hoards the things it ought to throw away, it treasures the things that ought to be forgotten. So he attempts to free himself from the dead hand of the past and to overcome any obstacle that would prevent him from living as he should. The Christian life is a race, and in any race, the runner must not allow his attention to be diverted by anything off course; distractions are fatal, as Atalanta learned to her cost. What then are the things that those who run the Christian race ought to forget?

Past Attainments

In the Hebrew original, Psalm 45 bears the title "A Love Song." It was probably composed and recited by a court poet on the occasion of the ruler's wedding. We do not know which Israelite king is being referred to in the first verse — Solomon, Ahab, and Jehu have all been suggested. As the new queen takes her place in the harem she is bidden to turn her back on the past:

> Listen, my daughter, hear my words
>   and consider them:

> forget your own people and your father's house;
> and, when the king desires your beauty,
>> remember that he is your lord. (vv. 10-11)

Such a request points to her foreign birth and calls on her to break all old ties, both cultural and religious. When one recalls the headache that Solomon's foreign wives (all seven hundred of them) and Ahab's Jezebel caused the biblical authors because they brought their pagan practices with them, the request is hardly surprising. But it could not have been easy for the queen. She was being asked to renounce what she valued, to "forget" what she considered to have been of importance in her past life, and to cast aside all that she had attained and achieved.

Christian discipleship may be viewed in much the same way. For a few years, I was privileged to teach in an Anglican theological college. The students had chosen a particular form of the Christian life, and in doing so had deliberately rejected other possibilities. They came to college with considerable achievements behind them: a responsible job at which they were successful, academic qualifications with the possibility of gaining some more, the development of some particular talent that had given others pleasure and commanded their respect, a position of trust in the local community or the parish church. Every one of them could think of some material attainment in the secular world. And it was important that they should, for surely they were not seeking ordination because they had been misfits elsewhere; admission to the ministry on that ticket would have been a recipe for disaster. It was important that their curriculum vitae offered proof of some attainment. They needed to have a positive self-esteem. With ordination they did not lose their talent or their ability to achieve. Their abilities would be channeled into different areas, but they would still be there.

Most of us need only look back into last week to feel

satisfied with some particular achievement. Apart from material attainments, there are spiritual ones. We may have been of help to another person in a dark hour simply because we were prepared to be open and sympathetic. We may feel that through prayer and counsel we are getting the better of some personal trait that makes life a strain for those about us.

Such achievements should not, of course, be devalued. They should be remembered with thankfulness and used to instruct the present. Like the psalmist we pray that we may use past experiences profitably: "Teach us to number our days that we may apply our hearts unto wisdom" (Ps. 90:12). But if our attainments suggest to us that little more remains to be done, we should forget them. If they make us think that we have traveled along one particular road far enough and that we can now afford to stop, we should forget them. If they lead to a sense of self-satisfaction and leave us with no further aspirations, we should forget them. It has been well said that "some people's chains are to be found in their achievements." If we are not careful, our attainments can make us self-centered and lead us to feel superior and smug. The Bible suggests that we should be more intent on what we may become than on what we are. In Paul's words, "For his sake I have suffered the loss of all things, and count them as refuse in order that I may gain Christ." The apostle refuses to make his achievements the foundation of his self-esteem, for he can now see how insignificant those things are that he once prized so highly. In the words of Voltaire, "the good must give way to the better."

Past Failures

The Jews in the time of Jesus interpreted Psalm 45 in a non-literal or allegorical sense. The theme was the nation's loyalty to God; the king was the Messiah and the bride was Israel. From the Letter to the Hebrews (1:8-9) we see that the first Christians followed this lead. The author of Hebrews believes that Christ is being addressed in verses 6 and 7 of the psalm:

> Your throne is like God's throne, eternal,
>   your royal sceptre a sceptre of righteousness.
> You have loved right and hated wrong;
> so God, your God, has anointed you
>   above your fellows with oil, the token of joy.

In this nonliteral sense the psalm was regarded by the early Church as being concerned with discipleship. The followers of Christ were exhorted to forget the past and concentrate on the new relationship they had just formed. They were new beings, born again through water and the spirit. This meant that the failures of the past were swept away and the slate wiped clean.

The same is true today. But for some, past failures are not easily pushed into the background. And this is a pity, for the memory of a failure can undermine any new attempt. For instance, those who have failed in some way often expect, though unconsciously, to fail again. Because they have submitted to some temptation in the past, they will convince themselves that that is the way they are made and that they will never do any better. Another example is the sin that, although forgiven, refuses to be blotted out. "Living with guilt" can present great problems for many people.[1]

Some may respond to this by saying that they do not have these feelings of guilt, that they are in no way obsessed by

---

1. For much of what follows I am indebted to H. McKeating, *Living with Guilt* (London: SCM, 1970).

them. Well, if they feel like that, they may be assured that there are many people like them. Guilt feelings are not their problem. But any counselor is only too well aware of those who are plagued by guilt: people who just cannot or will not forget past failures, and as a result suffer from very low self-esteem. Many Christians are among them, and mental hospitals have their fair share of them. In a book written jointly by an Anglican priest and a psychologist we read:

> It seems that much human misery centres around failure to value ourselves and finds its extreme in suicide and self-destructive behaviour. Christians are not exempt from this experience. Some may feed their own negative self-esteem by an excessive appeal to Scriptural passages that emphasise sin, guilt and alienation. Others may find that negative self-esteem is reinforced by a church culture that majors on criticism and exhortation from the pulpit rather than on affirmation.[2]

Individuals' inability to keep high standards by their own unaided efforts is often emphasized in Christian teaching.

Evidence that the Bible was aware of the problem that living with guilt can cause is to be found in the Book of Leviticus. In chapter 6 the author lists various transgressions and stipulates how restitution must be made. "If any person sins and commits a grievous fault against the Lord, whether he lies to a fellow-countryman about a deposit or contract, or a theft, or wrongs him by extortion, or finds lost property and lies about it" (6:1-3), he must compensate the man he has offended by giving back the stolen goods and adding a surcharge of 20 percent. But that is not all. In order to make full amends he must bring to the priest

---

2. J. and A. McGrath, *The Dilemma of Self-Esteem* (Cambridge: Crossways, 1992), p. 83.

a ram or its equivalent as a reparation offering. In other words the sin has a spiritual as well as a social dimension. When the transgressor has done all that can reasonably be expected of him to compensate for his crime, some form of guilt is felt to remain, which can be expiated only by means of sacrifice. He will not fail to remember his sin, especially since he had to pay 20 percent, but the sacrificial system offered him the means whereby he could deliberately push it aside.

For Christians the same thing happens in the sacrament of reconciliation. It exhorts them never to allow the past to limit their hopes of future possibilities or to undermine their confidence in future victories. They are people who are unfettered by the past. They can look it squarely in the face, but be neither resentful nor embittered. They begin each day anew, having written off the failures of yesterday. They know of them and are penitent about them, but they are not swamped by them. They know they have failed and that they will fail again. Yet they are free of failure; free of its effects and free of its power. This is the real meaning of absolution. It is not an accident that the western Christian tradition has framed its presentation of the gospel almost exclusively in terms of sin and forgiveness.

> He died that we might be forgiven;
> He died to make us good,
> That we might go at last to heaven
> Saved by his precious blood.

Past Injuries

It would surely be a great blessing if we could forget the injuries done to us. For every injury is aggravated by remembrance.

This sense of aggravation is most keenly felt where a number of people live at close quarters, whether it be in a family, a place of work, or a religious community. I choose this particular milieu to talk about injuries for three reasons. The first is the commitment involved. If there is a disagreement at the tennis club we can take our membership elsewhere. If we do not see eye to eye with the rector we can try another parish. But if relations in the family, the office, or the community become strained, we cannot just turn our back on the problem. We have to face the issue and learn to live with one another. Secondly, any close, and therefore demanding, relationship will ruthlessly expose our weaknesses. The family or community is the place where our shortcomings are most obvious. Those who associate with us on a daily basis see us at our best, but they also see us at our worst. Finally, a family or community, perhaps to a lesser extent a colleague, is prepared to come to terms with our failings. In the very place where we are made most conscious of our weaknesses we find those who are willing to accept us as we are.

Such a community is a forgiving community — a community that forgets past injuries, in the biblical sense of deliberately pushing them aside. In this sense forgiveness contains a very positive element. It does not pretend that the offense does not matter, nor that it never happened. We can't erase what we said in a fit of pique; we can't cancel a disdainful look or an impatient gesture. To be reconciled is not to deny that we said it or claim that we didn't really mean it. To be reconciled is to go on in honesty, each knowing how the other sometimes feels, but not allowing that knowledge to embitter the relationship.

What is changed by this experience of reconciliation? The past certainly is not changed. In one sense a past injury will always be remembered. What is changed is some of the results

178

of the past. What is changed is the significance of the past. What we can change is what we let the past do to us. We may have been hurt, and that certainly matters, but what matters most is how we let the injury affect us. Forgiveness must contain a strong element of what the Bible means by forgetting — the deliberate rejection of the past in the interests of the future. A modern hymn puts it thus:

> Forgive our sins as we forgive
> You taught us, Lord, to pray;
> But you alone can grant us grace
> To live the words we say.
>
> How can your pardon reach and bless
> The unforgiving heart
> That broods on wrongs, and will not let
> Old bitterness depart?
>
> Lord cleanse the depths within our souls,
> And bid resentment cease;
> Then reconciled to God and man
> Our lives will spread your peace.

Forgetting achievements, failures, injuries, deliberately ignoring the apples strewn on the path, the Christian, like every runner in a race, does not count the laps that are past, only those that remain.

Acceptable Worship

See that you do not refuse to hear the voice that speaks. Those who refused to hear the oracle speaking on earth found no escape; still less shall we escape if we refuse to hear the One who speaks from heaven. Then indeed his voice shook the earth, but now he has promised, "Yet once again I will shake not earth alone, but the heavens also." The words "once again" — and only once — imply that the shaking of these created things means their removal, and then what is not shaken will remain. The kingdom we are given is unshakable; let us therefore give thanks to God, and so worship him as he would be worshipped, with reverence and awe; for our God is a devouring fire.

Hebrews 12:25-29

THE AUTHOR OF THE LETTER TO THE HEBREWS was writing to a dispirited group of people who seem to have been on the point of renouncing their newfound faith. His readers had all but given up trying to fight the rotten paganism of the Roman Empire and were drifting away on the tide. Like careless mariners, they were in danger of being shipwrecked on the rocks.

Originally, this letter was a rope thrown out to the drifters to haul them back to the shore. The author, whose identity is not known, has a distinctive style: he alternates exposition of Scripture with warning and exhortation. Passages that expound the text of the Old Testament are followed by threats and appeals.

Because he is an extremely practical person, the writer is fully aware of the dangers facing true religion, one of which is the neglect of public worship. Although he has mentioned this issue previously, he introduces the topic again in the twelfth chapter by warning the Hebrews not to "refuse to hear the voice that speaks," a reference, presumably, to the voice of God in Jesus. He reminds them of what happened to the wilderness generation when it refused to listen to God communicating through Moses on Mount Sinai — "the oracle speaking on earth." Because Christians have been promised abiding realities that cannot be shaken, they should recognize such a privilege by offering worship that is acceptable to God. "Let us therefore give thanks to God, and so worship him as he would be worshipped, with reverence and awe." With this exhortation in mind, I want to consider some of the dimensions or characteristics of Christian worship in general and of the Anglican variety in particular.

Persistence

Worship, in every religion, is characterized by a certain stubbornness — it refuses to die out. It has survived, up to the present time, under the most adverse circumstances. As the Old Testament demonstrates, the worship of Jehovah was an integral part of the religion of ancient Israel. From the time of Solomon onwards, it was centered on the Jerusalem temple. Indeed, so central was the temple to Israelite worship that when

181

it was destroyed by Nebuchadnezzar early in the sixth century BC, the exiled inhabitants of Judah concluded that they no longer had access to God. As they sat by the rivers of Babylon, far from their ancestral homeland, the instruments of worship became redundant: "there on the willow-trees we hung up our harps." With the shock of exile, faith eroded. For the disillusioned captives, worship no longer made any sense because God was dead. Their plaintive response, when asked by their captors to sing some of the songs of Zion, is hardly surprising: "How could we sing the Lord's song in a foreign land?" (Ps. 137:2-4). Because God, in Israel's thinking, was confined to his own land, and because the temple could not be rebuilt anywhere but in Jerusalem, worship, as the people of Judah had known it, was at an end. But under the guidance of the great prophets of the period, Jeremiah, Ezekiel, and the Second Isaiah (Isaiah 40–55), the exiles rediscovered their faith and found that their God was in captivity with them. Despite the initial pessimism, Jewish worship survived and found a place in the Synagogue, where it continues until this day.

In the story of Christian origins also a prominent place is given to the survival of worship in the face of cruel persecution. A patient endurance and a determination to meet for worship, whatever the obstacles, were marks of the early Church. According to Acts 20:7-12, the Christian community at Troas in Asia Minor assembled weekly to break bread and to pray on the third floor of a private house, presumably to avoid harassment. When Christians began to experience life under Islam in the seventh century, they found that their witness was greatly restricted. It was forbidden, for example, to display any Christian symbol outside a church building; to this day, churches in Muslim countries are not marked by a cross. It was also forbidden to ring bells loudly to call the faithful to worship, which is why some Orthodox churches still use wooden clappers to mark the times of services. Members of Christian groups were subject to punitive taxation. They were even cruelly persecuted for professing their faith in Christ — as in some Islamic states they still are — while active proselytizing drew heavy penalties. The only activity open to Christians was worship, which is perhaps why in the Oriental Orthodox churches the celebration of the liturgy is such a lengthy process. Because it was the only means of witnessing permitted by law, worship came to be regarded as a very significant aspect of the Church's life. Its practitioners persisted, and as a result worship survived.

The diocese in which I am canonically resident was founded in the year 546, during what is referred to by historians of the Celtic Church as "the age of the saints." This was a period of expansion and growth, to which the many ancient churches still standing on the west coast of Wales bear witness. Despite repeated Viking raids from across the North Sea during the Dark Ages, those early worshiping communities not only survived but flourished, making a significant contribution to the propagation of the faith in these islands. Today that ancient Celtic heritage, which testifies to the persistence of worship against all odds, is being rediscovered.

In our own times, despite repeated attempts by hostile governments such as those of Albania, China, and Soviet Russia to proscribe its expression, worship has survived. During seventy years of repression and martyrdom in Eastern Europe, worshiping communities of Christians continued to meet. Soon after communism collapsed less than a decade ago, plans were made and vast amounts of money donated by Russia's *nouveaux riches* to rebuild Moscow's Cathedral of Christ the Savior, razed to the ground by Stalin. According to Canon Michael Bordeaux of the Keston Institute, which monitors Church life in the former Soviet Union, the Russian people are experiencing a dramatic revival in parish life. Clergy are exhausted by fundraising drives to repair ruined churches, by lengthy worship services, and by constant calls to baptize, marry, and bury. Parish activities such as Sunday schools, catechism classes, and youth clubs, suppressed for most of this century, are returning. To cope with this demand, forty new seminaries have recently been opened. Such a dramatic revival demonstrates that worship has persisted under the most adverse circumstances.

This persistence is to be found not only in the history books and under hostile regimes, it is also a very real dimension of contemporary church life. In every parish a weekly service of worship is still the focal point of congregational life. Various programs and projects, all of them worthwhile, come and go in response to the needs of the moment. But worship has remained. Whatever a church does or does not do, it will always assemble for worship. Sunday by Sunday the bell tolls to call the faithful to prayer, for celebrating the liturgy is the one constant element in the life of every parish. The significance of this continuity is nowhere more obvious than in an interregnum, when the congregation, through its representatives, strives to maintain, sometimes with difficulty, the regular round of prayer and praise.

Such persistence must indicate that worship has a hold on something deep in the human psyche, otherwise it would not have survived. In sounding the call to worship, the Church offers men and women the opportunity, amid the hustle and bustle of life, to look beyond themselves to the one who is infinite and eternal. Worship points us beyond the narrow limits of sight, touch, and hearing to the immeasurable arena of the spirit. Ideally it should bring us out of ourselves by engendering in us a sense of reverence and dependence.

Participation

One of the criticisms that the author of the Letter to the Hebrews levels at his readers is faithlessness. He regards apostasy as the supreme danger and exhorts his fellow Christians to ensure that no one among them becomes "a deserter from the living God" (3:12). In practical terms this refers to the deliberate abandonment of the Christian gospel by those who absent themselves from services of worship. "We ought to see how each of us may best arouse others to love and active goodness, not staying away from our meetings, as some do, but rather encouraging one another" (10:24f.). By stressing the importance of the congregation, the writer underlines the danger of choosing isolation instead of fellowship. He correctly concludes that falling away from the community of believers is the first step in falling away from the faith.

The famous evangelist D. L. Moody once called on a leading Chicago citizen to speak about Christian commitment. The two men were seated in the lounge where there was a coal fire burning in the grate. During the conversation Moody's host claimed that he need not join a church to be a Christian; he insisted that he could be just as committed to the cause of Christ outside the fellowship of worshipers and believers as he could be within it. Moody listened attentively but said nothing. After a few minutes he got up, stepped to the fireplace, and with a pair of tongs took out a live coal from the flames, placing it on the hearth by itself. In silence the two men watched it smolder and go out. Moody's host took the point and became an active churchman.

The truth that religious commitment implies membership of and participation in a community is corroborated time and time again in Scripture. It is almost always a group that God summons to serve and worship him, not separate individuals.

First it was Abraham and his family who were called to be the worshiping community. When he entered Canaan, the land promised to him and to his descendants by God, Abraham "built an altar to the Lord and invoked the Lord by name" (Gen. 12:8). Then came the twelve tribes, the sons of Jacob. Eventually the community comprised the whole of Israel, a people that was God's "special possession," his "kingdom of priests," his "'holy nation" (Ex. 19:5). Even great individualists such as Jeremiah and Amos, though critical of contemporary worship, never abandoned the group. In the New Testament there is but little mention of solitary Christians. The reference is almost always to the "saints," in the sense of the local church — whether it be in Rome, Corinth, Ephesus, or Philippi. Even Jesus, who hardly needed the support of public worship to sustain his relationship with God, identified himself totally with his own community in this respect. According to Mark, he opened his ministry with a Sabbath visit to the synagogue at Capernaum, where he "began to teach" (1:21). Luke also states in a significant aside that "he came to Nazareth, where he had been brought up, and went to synagogue on the Sabbath day as he regularly did" (4:16). At the outset of his ministry he chose twelve men who were the nucleus of what later became the Church and taught them to say *Our* Father." It is clear from the New Testament that no one ever considered being a Christian apart from the worshiping community. There were no loners, no isolated believers.

According to Christian tradition, therefore, worship implies participation in the sense of belonging to a specific group of like-minded people. But it also implies participation in the more obvious sense of "taking part" in acts of worship. This, of course, is nothing new for Anglicans. By 1999 Anglican congregations will have been participating in church services for four hundred and fifty years. But when it was first instituted by Thomas Cranmer in the sixteenth century, congregational participation in the liturgy was a novel idea. During the Middle Ages, when the distinction between clergy and laity was much more pronounced than it is today, the modern concept of the Church as "the people of God," gathering weekly around a common table, was entirely lacking. The medieval Church conveyed to the faithful the conviction that a sense of reverence and awe was more appropriate for the worshiper in God's house than a sense of community, a conviction that both architecture and liturgy served to demonstrate.

The church building was a "sermon in stone," in the sense that its design and layout reflected current theological thinking. A stone altar stood on an elevation against the east wall, separated from the nave by a rood screen that filled the chancel arch. The congregation, which was confined to the nave, was little more than a group of spectators watching the ceremonies performed at the altar by clergy and ministers. To be more precise, it was a group of listeners, for the screen of wood or stone that separated priest from people would usually be thick and heavy, with only a small opening. The faithful would attend church quite literally to "hear" Mass, not to join in the worship. They would watch and listen passively as the priest celebrated the liturgy standing before the altar with his back to them. The central service of the Church was not *shared* by those present but *heard*. It was an act of worship performed in the sanctuary by the clergy on behalf of the laity, not a corporate action in which the whole congregation participated. The priest's role was to represent his parishioners before God, not lead them in worship. In his authoritative study of Christian worship, *The Shape of the Liturgy,* Gregory Dix traces the baleful development of the Eucharist from being in the early centuries the concelebration of the people of God to something celebrated by the priest for the people. The very shape and contents of the church building gave credence to such theology.

But it was not only the architecture that undermined any sense of congregational worship; the fact that the liturgy was in Latin further discouraged participation. For even if they had been able to read, the worshipers would not have been able to understand most of what was being said. Moreover, the service books were complicated and difficult to follow even for those with sufficient education to be able to use them. Referring to this in the preface to his First Prayer Book of 1549, Thomas Cranmer states that "to turn the Book only was so hard and intricate a matter, that many times there was more business to find out what should be read, than to read it when it was found out."[1] The combination of a foreign tongue and an intricate service book crushed any possibility of having an instructed laity, well-educated in matters of faith.

Since their participation was not expected, the worshipers were free to move about the nave as they pleased (there would have been no pews) and engage in private devotion before statues of the saints while prayers were recited at the altar. Inattention and irreverence at Mass were common. The only point in the service at which the laity paid any attention to the proceedings was the moment at which, it was believed, the elements became the body and blood of Christ. As the priest spoke the words of institution over the bread and wine, and then raised the consecrated bread in an action known as "the elevation of the host," a bell would ring to call attention to this part of the consecration prayer. Since by the twelfth century the Mass was celebrated with no communicants at all except the priest (the congregation communicated only twice or at most three times a year), the moment of consecration and elevation became the climax of the service. For the worshiper

1. Quoted by D. E. W. Harrison and M. C. Sansom, *Worship in the Church of England* (London: SPCK, 1982), p. 31.

it was the most solemn part of the Mass, compared to which other aspects of the service mattered little.

A. G. Hebert regards the introduction of the noncommunicating Mass as "a profound change which radically altered the character of Christian worship" and quotes the opinion of the famous liturgical scholar Yves Brilioth to the effect that it was "the great disaster" in the history of the liturgy.[2] The objection of the liturgists to the prominence given to the act of consecration is that it shifted the service's center of gravity away from the communion, where, traditionally, it had been from the earliest times. Whereas St. Augustine in the fifth century states that the communion of the people is the consummation of the service, St. Thomas Aquinas, writing eight centuries later, claims that the action of the priest is the climax, with the communion of the people an optional addition. By the twelfth century the stress on congregational participation had been superseded by an emphasis on individual piety. As a result, the congregation became increasingly a collection of unrelated individuals meeting for a religious service.

Throughout the Middle Ages, therefore, architecture and liturgy ensured that the thought of participating in worship was foreign to the people in the pews. The corporate dimension of the liturgy, once a prominent feature of every service, was dissipated. Ordinary parishioners attending Sunday Mass would not have known that they were meant to share in the "common" prayer of a Christian community. They believed that all that was required of them was to listen to the "murmur of the Mass" and witness the elevation of the host. But our Anglican forefathers changed all that, or at least initiated the process of change. They emphasized the congregational nature

2. A. G. Hebert, *Liturgy and Society* (London: Faber and Faber, 1961), p. 1.

of worship, in the first instance, by taking seriously the place of liturgical assembly and rearranging the furniture. They were aware that the church buildings which they had inherited embodied an understanding of worship that they rejected. The two-roomed church, in which the nave was separated from the chancel and sanctuary by a screen and a flight of steps, was not suitable for the reformed worship they had in mind. In future the altar was to be made of wood, not stone, and covered with a fair linen cloth reaching to the ground on all four sides. In his injunctions of 1550 Bishop Ridley exhorted the clergy of the diocese of London "to erect and set up the Lord's Board, after the form of an honest table decently covered, in such place of the quire or chancel as shall be thought most meet."[3] Though Ridley's wish was that this portable altar should be placed in the chancel, the more radical reformers wanted it to be in the nave in full view of the congregation, and the priest instructed to stand behind it facing the people.

The conversion of ancient buildings to make them suitable for Anglican services is perhaps best encapsulated in the following quotation: "The process by which mediaeval churches were adapted for Prayer Book worship might be summed up as one of taking the communicants into the chancel for the Eucharist, so that they can be within sight and hearing of the priest at the altar; and of bringing down the priest from the chancel into the nave so that he could be amongst his people for Morning and Evening Prayer."[4] There was an unmistakable emphasis on lay participation, which was reflected in the ordering of the furniture. It must, however, be admitted that the Reformers did not go far enough with regard to the environ-

3. Quoted by C. W. Dugmore, *The Mass and the English Reformers* (London: Macmillan, 1958), p. 151.

4. G. W. O. Addleshaw and F. Etchells, *The Architectural Setting of Anglican Worship* (London: Faber and Faber, 1948), n. 45.

ment of worship. Despite high ideals, their efforts to correct the deformed piety of their predecessors did not issue in wholesale alterations of church buildings. The long, narrow chancel, with its rood screen and its high altar standing against the east wall, persisted, as the ecclesiastical architecture of Queen Victoria's Britain amply demonstrates. It is only in the second half of the twentieth century, as a result of the so-called Liturgical Movement, with its emphasis on worship as "the work of the people," that Anglican architecture has begun to reflect the dialogical character of worship to any great extent.

In England the man who did most to reform the liturgy was Thomas Cranmer. A linguist, historian, and theologian, he spared no effort in making the Mass a congregational act of worship on the pattern of the early Church. So that all present could understand the prayers and join the clergy in reciting them, he dropped Latin in favor of the vernacular. He encouraged everyone to take communion regularly in both kinds, thus allowing the congregation to participate fully in what was once again regarded as the consummation of the service. Last but not least, he simplified the services by providing the worshiper with one book instead of many.

Though Cranmer's Book of Common Prayer has not been without its critics, Anglicans may be justifiably proud of it, not least because it has permitted participation. Horton Davies comments thus on its uniqueness:

> The Book of Common Prayer is unique in being the first Book of *Common* Prayer, in that it has always been used both by priest and people, whereas previously priests had a different set of prayer books and the people had none, unless they were Latin scholars. Such a book has kept minister and people close in English life. It has encouraged the growth of a lay spirituality of depth. In yet another sense, the prayers of the Prayer Book

are *common* — that is, they have a richly responsive construction and character, whether in the Litany, or in the versicles and responses of the Suffrages, or in the general confessions, and elsewhere. This means that there has always been in Anglican worship a continuing dialogue between priest and people, an ongoing liturgical "conversation." This can be contrasted with the tyranny of the ministerial voice in Reformed worship, for the minister's is often the only voice heard in prayer, and the congregation is mute, and often says the permitted "Amen" with little conviction.[5]

The prayer book emphasizes that Christian worship is a participatory event.

But the use of a common prayer book is not the only means of involving the laity in services; the singing of hymns is another, very significant, method. Singing well-known hymns is one of the few corporate Christian activities that are successful. While hymn singing was confined during the Middle Ages to monks and those who sang the Mass, at the Reformation it became a congregational activity. Indeed, in some churches of the Reformed tradition it remained for centuries the only active way in which worshipers participated in the services. Although Cranmer himself made no provision for hymns in his first two prayer books (1549 and 1552), the revision made in 1559, after his death, contained a Royal Injunction of Queen Elizabeth I to the effect that a "hymn or such-like song" should be sung at Morning or Evening Prayer. Originally hymns were intended as supplements to the prayer book, but within a few years the metrical psalm was a regular ingredient of Anglican worship, and by the nineteenth century

5. Horton Davies, *Worship and Theology in England: From Cranmer to Hooker 1534–1603* (Princeton: Princeton University Press, 1970), p. 225.

hymns had become fully integrated into church services. They enabled the worshiper to participate physically in the liturgy.

Propriety

The title of this chapter might give the impression that the phrase "acceptable worship" meant worship that was acceptable to *us*. But that is not what it means. The author of the Letter to the Hebrews is referring to that which is acceptable to *God*. Some translations make this clear: "Let us give thanks to God, and so worship him as he would be worshiped"; "Let us worship in a manner well pleasing to God." But the correct translation does not make the issue any easier to handle. For we immediately assume that if we like a particular method of worship, God also must like it. That is, we consider that which is acceptable to God to be whatever is acceptable to us. Furthermore, in worship there is a markedly subjective element. In other words, we deem to be the right and proper form of public worship that which is endorsed by our own church or denomination and which we particularly enjoy. Up to 1965 the Roman Catholic Church insisted that Latin was the only acceptable liturgical language. There are Anglicans who are wedded to the "incomparable liturgy" of the Book of Common Prayer of 1662. For the Orthodox churches the liturgy is not worth having unless it lasts three hours. The Salvation Army insists on hymns with everything, while the Baptist feels cheated if the sermon lasts less than forty minutes. Opinions about the acceptability or propriety of worship vary greatly, despite a correct understanding of the biblical text.

This highly subjective element contributes to making public worship a veritable minefield for those whose task it is to order it. In no other area is it easier to become convinced that our personal whims amount to fundamental principles than in this one. There is a simple reason for this: namely, that we are all expert liturgists — or at least we believe ourselves to be. We may not be able to claim expertise in the Old Testament because we never enrolled in the Hebrew class when we were in college. And since our Greek is not what it used to be, we cannot regard ourselves as New Testament pundits either. We might consider ourselves knowledgeable about the history of the Church, until someone catches us out with the date of the Council of Constantinople. But worship is different. We are all expert liturgists, ready to pronounce judgment at a moment's notice. In matters liturgical, every one of us has consultancy status.

If this is difficult to believe, apply a few simple tests. Try introducing some new hymns, or a different translation of the Bible, or, God forbid, a revised prayer book, and wait for the "experts" to make a pronouncement. Try moving the furniture or changing the times of services, and see the hackles rise. In most cases opposition to change is based on custom and individual preference, not on reasoned argument. Adherence to tradition is defended by means of "the seven last words" that stifle further discussion: "That's the way we've always done it." And because their arguments are based on emotion rather than on principles, people can sulk indefinitely if their concept of acceptable worship is undermined. They will even withdraw their membership from a congregation that has been their spiritual home for as long as they can remember and become a pain in the neck somewhere else.

There is a certain arrogance in an attitude that says, "If the worship that I attend is not precisely what I want, then I can justifiably feel aggrieved." In liturgical matters, as in others, there is a need for humility, the humility that accepts what other people want, though it may not be entirely to our liking. This does not mean that we should swallow uncritically what we genuinely believe to be substandard and sloppy. High standards must be upheld in liturgy as in everything else. The propriety of worship requires careful monitoring for a variety of reasons, one of which is that the Sunday service is every parish's shop window. People looking for a spiritual home do not make their first contact with a congregation by attending the men's breakfast, or the Bible study group, or a meeting of the altar guild. They come to church on a Sunday morning. What happens during the service is crucial, since it can determine whether the casual visitor returns or not. In other words, the average parish has sixty minutes a week in which to attract new members; it has an hour to create addicts. A celebration of the liturgy should end in a sense of mission. Therefore, because worship is vital to the life of the Church, it requires careful assessment in accordance with specific liturgical principles. But when judgments are made, humility and constructive criticism should be held in tension.

What are the criteria that should be used to define the acceptability of Anglican worship? There are at least two: stability and vitality. From the earliest times, Christian worship has followed a prescribed order, the essence of which has been a combination of word and sacrament. These two constants, which encourage the worshipers to identify themselves with a continuing community of faith, have stood the test of time, though the balance between them has varied greatly from one branch of Christ's Church to another. Traditionally, Protestants have emphasized the former, regarding the sermon as the climax of the service, while Catholics have emphasized the latter. Modern Anglican liturgies attempt to strike the correct balance. These two permanent ingredients provide the Eucharist with a stable framework that allows worshipers to concentrate on what they are doing; they are not always wondering what may be coming next. But because the liturgy contains no surprises, it

195

has been criticized for being formal, a word that carries over-tones of boredom and insincerity. Though the very real dangers of formality in worship should be heeded, the advantages of having a prescribed form should also be recognized.

One way of appreciating the fixed form is to attempt to draw up an order of service from scratch. Faced with a blank sheet of paper, one quickly appreciates the difficulty of such a task. To produce a good act of worship, much thought and care must be put into the planning and construction of it. A permanent framework, which is fashioned according to clear liturgical principles and into which one's own contribution may be inserted, is surely a great boon. Most of us are not capable of expressing ourselves in any coherent way; we need the genius of the poet or the musician to do the job for us. The expert liturgist can say what we believe and feel far better than we can.

But the stability of the fixed form has a further advantage: it helps to protect Christian liturgy from fake gurus and reli-gious charlatans who con gullible congregations into partici-pating in acts of worship that are of doubtful validity. The fixed ritual exercises a tight control of the individual. Because the mode of worship is prescribed, the congregation is never at the mercy of some bright spark with a new idea. It is when they lose sight of tried and tested forms of worship, which link them with the faithful down the ages, that respectable suburbanites fall for the hocus-pocus passed off as praise by some new religious movements. Solid middle-class congregations can be persuaded to speak in tongues and jive for Jesus under flashing lights and occult symbols if the liturgical principles enshrined in historic forms of worship are disregarded.

But in spite of the stability it provides, one must admit that a formal liturgical service does not always evoke a sense of worship in the participants. A fixed form that varies little from week to week may well lack vitality; that which gives it life can be missing. It is always possible to plough through a set liturgy without ever allowing it to touch the heart. To be acceptable to us, and presumably to God, worship must be touched by the vital. It must possess that element of "magic," that indefinable "something," which elicits appreciative comments from those present. Clergy often cringe at being told by members of their congregation that they have "enjoyed" a service, especially if the sermon was particularly hard-hitting! It is true that an act of worship is not meant to be entertainment, but there is surely no reason why participants should not find it enjoyable. A fixed form of worship that is presented with dignity and decorum, in which the prayers are relevant to the needs of the community, the sermon intelligible and uplifting, and the hymns chosen with care, will bring satisfaction, even enjoyment, to those present.

ey